Colour

Manchester University Press

Cinema Aesthetics

Series editors Des O'Rawe and Sam Rohdie

Since the 1970s, many academics and teachers have been taking the study of film out of Film Studies by producing curricula and critical literature hostile to notions of artistic endeavour and aesthetic value. An old heresy is a new orthodoxy, and the argument that the cinema exists solely to illustrate the politics of culture, identity and pleasure is no longer an argument; it is now a 'core doctrine' of film education, particularly in the UK and the US. The Cinema Aesthetics series aims to challenge this orthodoxy by publishing visually literate and intellectually creative studies that explore a specific term, critical category, or interdisciplinary issue.

Also available

Stefania Parigi *Cinema – Italy* (ed. Sam Rohdie and Des O'Rawe; trans. Sam Rohdie)

Sam Rohdie *Montage*

Colour

Steven Peacock

Manchester University Press

Manchester and New York

distributed in the United States exclusively by Palgrave Macmillan

Published by Manchester University Press
Oxford Road, Manchester M13 9NR, UK
and Room 400, 175 Fifth Avenue, New York, NY 10010, USA
www.manchesteruniversitypress.co.uk

Distributed exclusively in the USA by
Palgrave Macmillan, 175 Fifth Avenue, New York,
NY 10010, USA

Distributed exclusively in Canada by
UBC Press, University of British Columbia, 2029 West Mall,
Vancouver, BC, Canada V6T 1Z2

British Library Cataloguing-in-Publication Data
A catalogue record for this book is available from the British Library

Library of Congress Cataloging-in-Publication Data applied for

ISBN 978 0 7190 7642 8 *hardback*
ISBN 978 0 7190 7643 5 *paperback*

First published 2010

Typeset in Scala and Scala Sans display by
Koinonia, Manchester
Printed in Great Britain
by the MPG Book Group

The purest and most thoughtful minds are those which love colour the most.
John Ruskin

With the exception of Eddie and myself, whom you already know, we're going to be using aliases on this job. Under no circumstances do I want any one of you to relate to each other by your Christian names, and I don't want any talk about yourself personally. That includes where you've been, your wife's name, where you might've done time, or maybe a bank you robbed in St Petersburg. All I want you guys to talk about, if you have to, is what you're going to do. That should do it. Here are your names.
Quentin Tarantino

I holiday in increments. In colours.
Markus Zusak

Contents

List of plates

Colour plates appear between pp. 82 and 83.

List of figures

Preface

Film writing has rather overlooked cinematic colour. At the time of this monograph's publication, the academic discipline of Film Studies is just beginning to realise the potential of sustained interest in and on colour. In light of prior absences and an emergent field of scholarship, this short book comes about through a desire to advance a critical, rather than theoretical, approach. It offers close readings of colour in a selection of films, from a wide range of times and countries.

In a scrutiny of cinematic moments, and when colour comes to the fore, films open up in new ways. From chapter to chapter, the book explores a spectrum of colourful applications. It starts by considering films that use colour in sparing amounts, and moves on to discuss increasingly abundant displays.

The study focuses on a few films' shifting patterns of colour, on repetitions, variations, and overlaps of meaning. While highlighting the use of colour, it also considers the connections between different stylistic elements such as camerawork, editing, performance, music, and lighting. Thinking about film's ability to place colour in a shifting relationship with all other points of style is crucial to our understanding of cinema aesthetics. Interpretation details the depth of integration that certain films achieve.

I have chosen to consider films that in different ways concern themselves with the workings of specific colours in the world, and in their worlds. The significance of these films emerges in colour. I hope that the reader will enjoy the interpretations, return to the films, and, above all, will develop the study of cinematic colour by exploring other films in this manner.

Acknowledgements

I want to thank the *Cinema Aesthetics* series editors, Des O'Rawe and Sam Rohdie, for their support and feedback, and for creating, in the series, an innovative, liberated approach to film criticism. Thank you to Matthew Frost for your belief in the project, trust, and patience. Thanks all round to colleagues and friends Andrew Klevan, Sarah Cardwell, Claire Hines, Darren Kerr, Alex Clayton, David Turner, and Thalia Baldwin. I am grateful to David Scorey and Matthew Roach for the generosity of their time and many conversations. To Henry and Dan: the boys. I thank the University of Hertfordshire for funding the project in its final stages. This project was supported by Southampton Solent University's Centre for Advanced Scholarship in Art and Design's Capability Fund, HEFCE. My students' observations in seminars have helped enhance the work and give continual inspiration.

This book is dedicated to Leigh.

Introduction

There is a moment in Eric Rohmer's *The Green Ray* (*Le Rayon vert*: 1986) that is suggestive of the main character's hesitancy about holidays. Delphine, played by Marie Rivière, visits her sister's family, asking after their summer plans. Her sister Babie invites her to accompany them to Ireland. Delphine's response is uncertain. She dallies with the idea, but also intimates that it doesn't quite meet her ideal ('But in August I want to see the sea, to swim'). One of Babie's young children is perched on Delphine's knee. Whilst distractedly answering her sister, Delphine makes a fuss of her fidgety niece, straightening the little girl's outfit and smoothing her hair. She does the same with her own neckline, her hand dabbing around the broad collar of her pale blue sweater. Then, as she loosely entertains the idea of holidaying, Delphine idly twirls a canary-yellow feather, brushing it under her chin [see plate 1]. Thoughts of going on holiday tickle her, irritating and diverting in their appeals. At the same time, for this character, such plans are only enjoyable when they are as loose and light as a pastel pullover and a feather. By firmly committing to a break, the pleasures of possibility constrict. Boldness becomes uncomfortable.

The following remarks on colour address a hesitation in Film Studies to engage with this stylistic element. At the time of writing, there appear only a handful of other books in the English language that focus on the subject. Steve Neale's *Cinema and Technology: Image, Sound, Colour* remains a keystone work, considering colour's development alongside other technological advancements of film.[1] Angela Dalle Vacche and Brian Price's edited collection *Color: the Film Reader* presents a set of historically significant writings (by, amongst others, Rudolf Arnheim, Sergei Eisenstein, and Natalie M. Kalmus).[2] Another edited collection, by Wendy Everett, asks theoretical questions of colour.[3] Scott Higgins' work focuses on the impact of Technicolor in the 1930s.[4] *Colour* is the first contemporary monograph to deal with the close criticism of film colour across decades and countries.

Though central to the plastics of cinema, colour often goes unacknowledged. As Richard Dyer attests, 'the reading of non-representational signs in the cinema is particularly under-developed'.[5] Under the banner of non-representational signs, Dyer lists colour first, alongside 'texture, movement, rhythm, melody, camerawork.'[6] As colour can appear uneasily abstract, existing only as a property of an object, it keeps getting missed, or subsumed into broader categories of film style. Such an elision occurs in David Bordwell and Kristin Thompson's definition of mise-en-scène, in which they highlight 'setting, lighting, costume, and the behaviour of the figures'.[7] Perhaps as we are now so familiar with seeing colour in movies (and movies in colour), expecting its appearance in most narrative film of all kinds, we forget to pay it attention. When colour occasionally emerges in academic writing, there is sometimes a jolt in the response towards theory, away from an experiential commitment to the element. This problematic point of style is held at a distance, regarded with disdain and distrust.[8] As Stephen Melville proclaims:

> Colour can seem bottomlessly resistant to nomination, attaching itself absolutely to its own specificity and the surfaces on which it has or finds its visibility, even as it also appears subject to endless alteration arising through its juxtaposition with other colours. Subjective and objective, physically fixed

and culturally constructed, absolutely proper and endlessly displaced, colour can appear as an unthinkable scandal.[9]

Rife with complexities, 'subject to endless alteration', colour resists critical classification. In turn, its challenges are often passed up (in avoidance, perhaps, of connections with a 'scandal').

As well as focusing on colour, this book offers an alternative to national, socio-political, and historically chronological approaches to film style. The choice of films (from around the world and different decades) depends on their particular handling of colour. It is a central aim of the book that the decision to mix works in fresh combinations will invigorate the study of colour, and encourage new ways of considering individual films, classical and contemporary, acclaimed or otherwise. Whilst the selected films may share resemblances in their palettes, their particularity is of most importance. Personal experiences of colour direct the criticism that follows, shaping the contours of debate. The study moves away from set denominations of specific colours in film, such as 'red = passion or danger'. It seeks instead to be more sensitive to shifting patterns of meaning found in colour, from film to film, and from moment to moment in a film.

One of the guiding principles of close criticism is to invite the reader-as-viewer to test his or her responses against those presented, to check his or her own understanding and experience of a given moment of film. In turn, it is important to establish that we are concerned with, as far as possible, an equivalent version of the same film. I list the full DVD titles and information in Appendix A. To allow the reader to compare a reading of colour with a still image of the moment under discussion, the book includes a section of colour plates. Some black-and-white stills also appear across the chapters, placed alongside passages of writing that touch on other aspects of a film sequence. Appendix B offers the reader a concise timeline of film colour's historical development, noting key technological and institutional processes, and the release of influential works, from early cinema to the digital age. Many of the later films listed in the timeline are included without explanation for their being there. It is hoped that the reader might return to some of these works with a renewed interest, to judge their often-lauded colourful applications as, for example, overbearing, irresolute, or brilliant.

To give space to the intricacies and complexities of colour on display in exemplary works, the book focuses on six films. The films are (in order of appearance) *Three Colours: White* (*Trzy Kolory: Biały*, Krzysztof Kieślowski: 1994 France/ Poland); *Equinox Flower* (*Higanbana*, Yasujiro Ozu: 1958 Japan); *The Green Ray* (*Le Rayon vert*, Eric Rohmer: 1986 France); *Written on the Wind* (Douglas Sirk: 1956 US); *Fear Eats the Soul* (*Angst essen Seele auf*, Rainer Werner Fassbinder: 1974 Germany); and *The Umbrellas of Cherbourg* (*Les Parapluies de Cherbourg*, Jacques Demy: 1964 France).

In turn, the six films present chromatic measures moving from understatement to amplification. Leading from one end of narrative cinema's colour spectrum, Chapter 1 examines *Three Colours: White*. While a colour film (and so not black-and-white), it offers a concentration of and on whiteness. Presenting a world immersed in this neutral colour, it is thoughtful about aspects of absorption and detachment. Dealing with divorce and faked deaths, *Three Colours: White* is a black comedy of complex restraint. Chapter 2 explores a film that is similarly restrained and concerned with reservation. *Equinox Flower* is a gentle comedy, addressing different attitudes across families and generations to marriage. As Ozu's first film in colour, *Equinox Flower* represents a cautious movement away from monochrome. Predominantly black-and-white designs combine with small amounts of colour from a limited range, particularly dashes of red. A father slowly accommodates his daughter's marital wishes. Bringing style and story together, the film explores the fragile meeting points of traditional and modern ways.

From red dabs to pastel washes: Chapter 3 progresses ideas raised in this introduction's first paragraph, exploring how, in *The Green Ray*, delicate colours accrue to convey a fragile sensibility. Rohmer's film applies a pale palette to express its protagonist's indeterminacy. Like the film, the chapter collects impressionistic sketches of transitional moments. Concentrating on visual designs, it also counters a critical tendency to focus on the abundant dialogue in Rohmer's works, on their 'verbal excess'.[10] *The Green Ray* achieves ambiguous and ambivalent suggestions of feeling in colour, expressive of 'the contrast or conflict between our thoughts or desires and our actions'.[11] The reading joins only a small group of critical responses in the English language to this film and director, and an even smaller set of works that holds attention on implications of a particular point of Rohmer's style.[12]

In contrast to the previous films' different kinds of restraint, intensity comes to the fore in Chapter 4, in *Written on the Wind*. Pitched to meet the melodramatic form, Technicolor schemes fill the film. The wealth of opulent colours on display befits a saga of being rich and lush. A brash palette moves beyond the seemingly crude morality tale of the film's story, developing intricate motifs and deepening the psychological complexities of characters. In painting a brightly extravagant world, the film sustains a heightened register. Many scholars of Sirk take such pronounced displays of stylisation as melodramatic 'excesses.'[13] This study sees the declamatory arrangements of colour characterising emotional intensity and more subtle appeals. Chapter 5 considers the resemblances, after Sirk's work, of a film by Rainer Werner Fassbinder. As part of a process of drawing on, intensifying and reshaping Sirk's visual language, Fassbinder's use of colour is crucial to the realisation of singularly confrontational cinema. Squaring up to the concentrations of Fassbinder's forceful aesthetic, the fifth chapter tackles one sequence and one colour in *Fear Eats the Soul*.

Chapter 6 addresses *The Umbrellas of Cherbourg* as a multicoloured fantasia of the everyday. Combining traits of the classical Hollywood musical, opera, operetta, and a painterly fascination with colour, the film creates bright dreamscapes in humdrum settings. The music, story, and colour combine and clash in surprising ways in this film, in shifting forms of the 'style-subject economy'.[4] In turn, *The Umbrellas of Cherbourg* develops narrative-led colour coding and more abstract applications.

In each of the chapters and instances, in looking closely at colour, the readings take account of the fine-grain distinctions within the films themselves. It is hoped that in selecting wide-ranging works, in attending to their individual, multi-dimensional appeals, the interpretations go some way to suggesting the prismatic nature of colour in film. In turn, a more extensive critical vocabulary can be developed, refined, and applied. As John Gage suggests, 'Colour-vocabularies seem to work with a very limited set of "basic" or "primary" terms.'[5] This book looks for language matching the rhetoric of the films under scrutiny. It notes and moves beyond generally inscribed meanings of certain colours, paying attention to shifting connections and comparisons. That is not to say it ignores particular cultural signifiers (such as the relationship of red to weddings in Japan, as explored in *Equinox Flower*). Rather, it views these deeply embedded associations as starting points, as shaded, embellished, and individualised by the films themselves.[16] The marker of colour's appearance in a film changes throughout, in varying relationships. As a crucial element of film style, it rewards responsive scrutiny.

1 *Three Colours: White* (Krzysztof Kieślowski: France/Poland, 1994)

'White has the appeal of the nothingness that is before birth, of the world in the ice age.'

(Wassily Kandinsky)[17]

'Everything is possible.'

(Mikolaj (Janusz Gajos), *Three Colours: White*)

Let's start with a blank sheet.

For Kieślowski, white suggests the potentiality for a new beginning, its blankness a *tabula rasa* ready for inscription through experience. As Kandinsky notes, white is 'pregnant with possibilities'.[18] In *Three Colours: White*, Kieślowski strips back the cinematic palette to a bleached state, combining white with greys and silvers in a washed-out world. Other colours appear – yellows, reds, greens, browns, and blues – but the whiteness predominates in each composition, by amount, placement, or visual emphasis. On a white canvas, the director paints, in layers, a cinematic portrait of lost souls. For the protagonists Karol Karol (Zbigniew Zamachowski), his estranged wife Dominique (Julie Delpy) and accidental cohort Mikolaj (Janusz Gajos), white trappings in the world create prospects of renewed freedom. *Three Colours: White*[19] is the perfect film to begin with, not only as it favours a mini-malist application of neutral colouring, but also as it presents a study of fresh starts.

At the same time, one might query the inclusion of *White* – a film that places such prominence on a 'non-colour' – in a book on colour. To cite Kandinsky again, 'White, although often considered as no colour (a theory largely due to the Impressionists, who saw no white in nature), is a symbol of the world from which all colour as a definite attribute has disappeared.'[20] Just as often though, theorists point to the fact that white contains every colour at once. As Hélio Oiticica suggests, 'White is the ideal colour-light, the synthesis-light of all colours.'[21] White brings the spectrum together and throws it back in a visual stimulation devoid of hue: a presence of sheer absence. The appearance of white and *White* raises vital questions about colour's constitution in and on film.

Immersing itself in the workings of one colour, the film orchestrates precise arrangements of white, reflecting in its blank surfaces the depth and complexities of thematic patterns. White's omnipresence makes the colour a character, dictating the tone and mood of the piece. Through the colour, the film develops particular expressions of psychological intensity and detachment. An all-consuming whiteness mirrors strong yet introspective emotional states: loneliness, self-pity, jealousy and the blankness of a hollowed-out life. *White* suggests that only at the point of nothingness will we find absolute parity, equality, and the will to begin again. Throughout the film, white's connotations snowball. In particular, the characters' lives play out in degrees of blankness and emptiness. The memory of a white wedding leads to disconnection and feeling nothing. Karol's ex-wife Dominique is coolly relentless in enacting her legally binding separation. Karol's assets become frozen and he has to sleep rough. The film considers the facts of 'having nothing' together with white's suggestions of bleakness and coldness. There are also, though, the prospects of new beginnings that come from complete erasure: a total whiteout. Developing these meditations on white's meanings, significance accrues around certain white settings, objects, and textures. Amongst others, these include concrete streets, snowy fields, coins, combs, birds, and a porcelain bust.

Just as colour can (as Melville suggests) 'seem bottomlessly resistant to nomination', the film closes with a gesture that both invites and resists the processes of interpretation. Bringing about his ex-wife's false imprisonment, Karol visits the jail. Through binoculars, he watches as Dominique signals the complexity of a love found only in disconnection. Wordlessly, locked away from her ex-husband, she makes a series of hand gestures, all oblique in meaning yet persuasively affecting. Karol's tears and a smile act as his silent acknowledgment. This couple can only understand togetherness through physical and emotional detachment. The hand gestures resist a simple union with signification. They are precious to just these two people precisely because they (the lovers, the gestures) are separated from direct association.

Presented in silence, the final gesture is reflective of white's eloquent muteness. Like the scenario of a prison locking up and setting free love because of separation, white's blankness keeps possibilities of connection alive precisely through

1.1 *Three Colours: White* (Krzysztof Kieślowski, 1994)

its lack of attachment. White is a void we fill with meaning yet remains, in its starkness, tantalisingly unknowable. In turn, according to Kieślowski's film, white offers the perfect visual metaphor for true love's paradox. We search to be close to another person, even as we know, in their separateness, that they are ultimately unreachable. To expand the earlier quotation of Kandinsky, 'White ... is a symbol of the world from which all as a definite attribute has disappeared. This world is too far above us for its harmony to touch our souls. A great silence, like an impenetrable wall, shrouds its life from our understanding. White, therefore, has this harmony of silence, which works upon us negatively, like many pauses in music that break temporarily the melody. It is not a dead

1.2 *Three Colours: White* (Krzysztof Kieślowski, 1994)

silence, but one pregnant with possibilities.'²² Love is a negotiation of another person's impenetrability that is in the end
unattainable (even in times of harmony, there will always
be a certain 'silence' between minds). We can connect these
ideas with Oiticica's understanding of white as, 'the most
static [of all colours], favouring silent, dense, metaphysical
duration.'²³ In step with these interpretations, Kieślowski's
film prefers metaphysical resonance to more sociologically
explicit associations of whiteness. Whereas film and Film
Studies predominantly offer treatises on the colour's politi-
cal or cultural significance, *White* remains silent.²⁴ This is
particularly unusual, given the ostensible brief of the *Three
Colours* trilogy.

The three films of the *Three Colours* trilogy are *Blue* (1993),
White (1994), and *Red* (1994). Taking the individual colours
of the French flag, each film embodies one of the associated values of 'liberté, égalité, and fraternité' that comprise
the country's revolutionary slogan. At the same time, the
films resist engaging in a direct exploration of socio-cultural
concerns that might appear essential to such a project. In
his monograph on the trilogy, Geoff Andrew suggests that
Kieślowski was 'insistent that his examination of the French
Revolutionary ideals of Liberty, Equality and Fraternity
should be understood in a personal, determinedly apolitical
sense.'²⁵ Although some socio-cultural references remain
– the central plot device of the 'Song for the Unification of
Europe' in *Blue*; the return to a capitalist European Union
Poland in *White*; the significance of the ferry and its drowned
dignitaries in the climactic moments of *Red* – the films form
an oblique, idiosyncratic triptych exploring the human condition and human relationships. The trilogy is more interested
in presenting meditations on loss, intimacy, and destiny than
mapping out the state of contemporary French society. The
flag's standards become universal.

An interest in intricate connections unites the three films.
The trilogy interweaves aspects of form (with specific colours
and characters appearing in all films but taking primary

position in one), narrative (through overarching plot strands and shared pivotal moments), and themes (concentrating on chance encounters, fatalism and the impact of death). These are films preoccupied with overlaps and intersections. As Tadeusz Szczepanski declares, 'Kieślowski ingeniously multiplies subtle refrains, parallelisms, counterpoints, correspondences, symmetries, echoes and mirror effects not only on the level of narrative threads, situations, characters or props in the roles of *res dramatica*, but also in *mise-en-scène*, use of colour, sound and ... music.'[26] A notable example of this fascination with parallelisms forms in the recurrent appearance of an elderly woman struggling to push empty bottles into an emerald green bottle bank. All of the three central protagonists across the trilogy bear witness to this bittersweet refrain on the human obligation to recycle. Each repeat sight draws viewer and character nearer to the task, closer to a little passing act of salvation (again, the will to begin again).

Above all, as a final binding connection, each film couples one colour with one female character. In this union, the trilogy creates three intimate portraits of separateness. The lives of three women are marked out in measures of physical and emotional isolation: in *Blue*, Julie (Juliette Binoche) mourns her recently deceased husband and son; in *White*, Dominique divorces Karol; in *Red*, Valentine (Irène Jacob) is increasingly captivated by eavesdropping on private conversations. In each film, the title colour associates closely with the main character's feelings. As Geoff Andrew suggests, in the first film of the trilogy, 'Blue ... is used not as a symbol of "freedom", but to create moods of melancholy and coldness, and to draw attention to the resonant emotional associations conjured up by objects and places in Julie's mind.'[27] Andrew interprets the colours in *Blue* as conveying Julie's 'intensely private responses to the world around her.'[28] These observations call to mind David Turner's argument in 'The Interiority of the Unknown Woman in Film':

1.3 *Three Colours: Blue* (Krzysztof Kieślowski, 1993)

1.4 *Three Colours: White* (Krzysztof Kieślowski, 1994)

1.5 *Three Colours: Red* (Krzysztof Kieślowski, 1994)

Film may be unable to consistently and elaborately specify
what a character is thinking or feeling, or to *verbally* represent the nature of a character's consciousness, but it does not
follow from this that film is incapable of subtle discriminations
regarding a character's mental life. Implication and suggestion
can provide far more than vague, impressionistic, 'emotional'
effects (albeit 'powerful' ones) ... we often discover much about
a character's interior life through the precise use of performance, camera position, editing, and so on. These discoveries,
though often the result of implication, suggestion, and evocation, can be (and often are) expressive of *particular* and *precise*
states of mind, as well as suggestive of broader notions, such
as the nature of a character's inner life.[29]

In the *Three Colours* trilogy, absorptions of colour suggest the
female characters' states of interiority. Through 'implication,
suggestion, and evocation', the three colours are individually expressive of three 'unknown' women's inner lives. The
absorptions make discriminations of thoughts and feelings,
and are expressive of emotional impenetrability: disclosing
and upholding the privacy of these characters' responses to
the world. *White* is different from the other two films as it
centres on the male character Karol, refracting Dominique's
unknown-ness through his responses to her detachment.

Alongside important aesthetic and expressive connections, there are key distinctions. The three films adopt (and
adapt) the conventions of different genres. *Blue* is a melodrama, *White* a black comedy, *Red* a mystery thriller (playing on similar conceits to Hitchcock's *Rear Window*). In their
handling of singularly predominant colours and in wider
stylistic strategies, the films also have their own unique
personalities. *Blue* operates with the most heightened register and in tonal extremes of melancholia, depression, and
euphoria. It has an intrusive style, with gushing impositions
of blue colouring matching the intense grief of a mourn-
ing wife. *Red*'s style arrests in a distinct manner. The film's
intense tone and rhythms reflect in supercharged red colouring. Crimson dashes match the protagonist's flare: a young,

hip photographer in the flash world of high fashion. The insistent presence of red becomes increasingly portentous. Urgency comes through in the strobe of red lights and the pulse of car alarms. A chance encounter with an old man changes the pace again, and slowly brings the stories of all three films together.

Stylistically, the middle section of the trilogy stands apart from its bookending counterparts. *White* follows the suggestions of its lead colour: bare, stripped down, lighter. It is less fond of saturations; the colourful handling of an orgasm is the only instance of overt stylisation in *White*. Unlike the other two films, it favours a naturalistic approach. There is a purveyance of white, but the density of colouring is the same as is naturally found in the world: in the snowy landscapes of Poland, concrete roadways, a white wedding dress, bird feathers, porcelain bowls. Arguably, while remaining opaque in its stance on such matters, *White* is the most politically explicit entry in the trilogy. As an exploration of equality, according to Andrew, 'the film derives much humour from its sardonic depiction of the dog-eat-dog mores of contemporary, capitalist Poland.'[30] Andrew continues by noting that, in *White*, 'social comment is ... a contextualising reflection of the emotional conflict between its two protagonists.'[31] While all three films have received positive responses from critics, *White* has had the least attention. This could be because of its restrained style, its middle position, or white's suggestions of emptiness. Neutral and compelling, *White*'s arrangements are there to be revealed and appreciated: written on.

Colour blocks

Initially, as the second work in the trilogy, the film wittily suggests how it manoeuvres around *Blue*. The first sequences follow Karol before, during, and after his divorce hearing at the Law Courts. At the back of the courtroom, the protagonist from *Blue* – Julie – appears in the doorway. As a harbour of justice, the Law Courts comprise a hub for all three

Where's the equality?

1.6 *Three Colours: White* (Krzysztof Kieślowski, 1994)

films, and all three values of French honour. The building's
portico spells out 'Liberté, Égalité, and Fraternité' in metre-
high engraving. The court officials unceremoniously turn
Julie away, and direct her outside. This is not her time. Her
dismissal heralds a concentration on white and Dominique's
different appeals.

White and greys wrap around our first sight of Karol as
he too gets past the designs of *Blue*. Cloaked in a seal-grey
overcoat, he trudges forwards along bleached flagstones.
Here as elsewhere in the film, light blanches his face and
skin to a wan pallor. The character carries a negative vibe,
appearing in his whiteness as a negative print of the world.
(Like a double negative, his name – Karol Karol – cancels
itself out.) As he heads to the divorce tribunal, suggestions of
impending separation fill the frame. Karol alone walks left to
right, against the flow of other passers-by. His broken French
is a little barrier to communication. Crucially, blue coloured
objects also form solid divisions. Blue railings jut between
Karol and the impressive austerity of the Courts building [see
plate 2]. He has to pause when a blue police van rolls in front
of him. As in the first film of the trilogy, blue appears to stand
in the way of the central character. In *Blue*, the colour represents an emotional blockade of shock and sadness. Unlike
that film's protagonist, Karol is able to overcome blue's
obstacles. He walks by the partitions, through the gateway to

the Law Courts, and steps around the police van. Although moving towards a situation in which his wife looks to lay down legal barriers between them, Karol finds a way of negotiating the obstructions around him. More precisely, as we shall see, physical blocks of whiteness will lead this character away from states of being blue, towards consolidation.

Staying firm

I'm interested here in exploring how the film conveys emotional impenetrability in densities of whiteness. Existing without shade or hue, white's essential solidness is fundamental to the film's concerns. The different physical consistencies of white things in the world are handled to express more graded qualities of emotional strength. Across the film, the two main characters work with white objects and against white surfaces of varying mass. Through these trappings, the couple find ways to become resilient to the other's separateness, and to connect. Objects stand in between them, or as conduits, channelling complexities of feeling.

The courtroom scene introduces Dominique. The sight is significant not only as the first of the film, but also as it emphasises her inflexibility. Instantly, *White* fixes (and fixes on, fixes in the mind) aspects of rigidity. The intimate details of the couple's marriage air in public, an awkward humiliation developing from bird droppings landing on Karol in front of the Courts. He enters the chambers. The stain on his coat draws attention to itself and invites comparison with the Judge's clean white lapel. A spot on Karol's person gives way to more ceremonial humiliations. The Court dispassionately examines the couple's love life, asking 'Was the marriage consummated that night?' Impotence emerges as a crucial factor in their break-up. The film explores many forms of powerlessness in human relationships. Here it hints at the importance of Karol being unable to engage sexually, to keep an erection (to 'stay hard'). It sets the suggestion against that of Dominique's stiffness.

1.7 *Three Colours: White* (Krzysztof Kieślowski, 1994)

1.8 *Three Colours: White* (Krzysztof Kieślowski, 1994)

1.9 *Three Colours: White* (Krzysztof Kieślowski, 1994)

A wide shot of the room reveals Dominique in the opposite dock to Karol. She stands under a series of globular white ceramic lights. The smooth elevated orbs are untouchable, fragile, and flawless in design. Under the spotlights, despite the open scrutiny of her marriage, Dominique shows no emotion. The film immediately presents her as distant and detached. Drawing nearer only accentuates the impression. In close shot and high lighting, the features of her face fix like those of an alabaster sculpture. Later, separated from his wife, Karol finds and cherishes a substitute for Dominique's impenetrability. A china bust stolen from a shop window presents Karol with another beautiful, hard profile of female grace. Cast in marble-white ceramic, the statuette replaces Dominique's own blank resistance.

The film contrasts past and present occasions in different textures of white things. In the courtroom scene, it cuts to a recurring flashback of Karol and Dominique at their wedding ceremony. The flashback resembles a memory in opaque white light and it is not clear who is remembering. In the haze, Dominique walks to the church door, the ceremony now complete. Enveloped in the white blooms of her wedding dress, she directs herself away from the camera's gaze. The dress's white veil floats across the frame. Flocks of pigeons flutter around her. In the flapping of soft white wings, a potentially romantic (or Romantic) vision contains more unsettling hints. Coming after the sight of Karol's stained coat, they are a bad omen, their appearance tainted by association. A crowd of guests throws white rice (as 'confetti') over the new bride. She finally turns around to face us. Just married, she stands alone. Even here, Karol is out of the picture. By withholding Dominique's face, turning her only at the last moment, the film emphasises suggestions of separation. Her veil is down, but the flapping birds and sprays of rice form other delicate white coverings in front of her eyes. While apparently a disclosure of a private memory, the flashback develops the sense of Dominique's detachment. Without fixed agency, like the veil and the dispersal of rice, the memory teases in its division. All three are insubstantial, and lightly hold her apart.

Coming out of the flashback and returning to the 'present', the film bleeds in the sound of the Court asking Karol to provide 'concrete reasons for wanting a divorce'. A blunt call for solid evidence replaces the flashback's flimsier appeals. We learn that Karol has been repeatedly unable to consummate the marriage. The Judge makes his final decision and declares the marriage annulled. A cut moves to a view of Karol throwing up into a white toilet bowl. The shock of the news registers in both a dislocating shift to a different setting and the retch. A bleaching glow of high-watt bulbs emphasises the sterility of the room and Karol's harsh new situation. The cold facts are glaring: as he can't 'get hard', his wife doesn't want to know. All of a sudden, his life hollows out. Emptying his stomach, Karol grips white-knuckled to the rim. From here on in, he will seek relief in rigid white objects.

Stonewall

In the aftermath of the divorce, the film immediately minimises human interaction around the character and sets up firm obstructions. At first, metal, plastic, and stonework block Karol's attempts to carry on. *White* pitches him out of the Courts and onto the streets to face the robotic anonymity of a cash machine. Karol puts in his card. Against a backdrop of white stone buildings, sallow light radiates from the computer screen. Bold white lettering blinks out stark instructions: ENTER YOUR CODE THEN PRESS VALIDATE. Under the divorce agreement, Karol's accounts are automatically frozen. His uncomprehending eyes reflect in the machine's screen. As a swiftly clipped edit moves the action inside the bank, metal scissors wielded by a faceless authority figure snip Karol's card in two. A gash of white light glints off the blades. In clear surfaces, blank stares and steely cuts, Karol is cancelled out. Homeless, Karol huddles to keep warm on the side of the road, his back against the wall. The

1.10 *Three Colours: White* (Krzysztof Kieślowski, 1994)

film allows itself a fleeting cold-hearted joke at his expense. The sight of the elderly woman at the bottle bank raises a wry smile for Karol. At the same time, a close shot places him against a graffiti tag sprayed on the side of the wall. A zero and an arrow point right at Karol. It is a blunt, stark-white sign of his bleak prospects. This man is nothing.

Hard luck

After a last ditch attempt at sexual reconciliation limply fails in Dominique's hair salon, Karol sets himself to becoming hardy. Character and film begin a process of consolidation around solidity. Falling on tough times, Karol finds steadfastness in white structures, settling for (and beside) everyday approximations of Dominique's resistance. First, he finds the china statuette by chance. Then, down in the subway, low on luck, Karol plays his silver comb for coins. He sets up camp under pallid strip-lights, against the porcelain sheen of the station's hard white tiles [see plate 3]. The fuzzy trumpeting of his comb echoes around the hollows – the solid surfaces of this space rebound sound. Even as he resigns himself to the slim pickings of a busker's life, he is now supported by the walls. At rock bottom, new opportunities emerge. A fellow Pole, Mikolaj, throws him a coin and stops to talk. Karol is sitting inside the suitcase (as he will travel,

later, back to Poland, under Mikolaj's supervision). Mikolaj
plucks at cylindrical towers of white papers – Karol's hairdressing diplomas – sticking out of the unlocked case. His
arrival opens a new page, replacing the importance of these
qualifications. (The papers will fall, unwanted, onto the railway tracks). As Mikolaj extends his invitation to return with
him to Poland, a piebald pigeon lands between them. An idea
of carefree flight comes into reach, a chance to get Karol out
of the muck, for good. However, Mikolaj also offers him a
dirty job, to kill someone. As Mikolaj makes his proposal,
the film again places Karol against the plain tiled surfaces
of the subway walls. At just this moment, the light hitting
the smooth facade mottles the tiles a sickly pea-green. The
instance of grim revelation is a good example of how the film
tints hard white forms to suggest a shifting frame of mind,
coloured by circumstance.

Contempt

Rigid white screens keep Dominique from Karol the final
time he sees and hears her in France. He is at once near to
and far from his wife's sexual advances. Spying Dominique in
silhouette clinches Karol's decision to escape and start again
in Poland, as well as forming an outline for the later, happier
encounter at the prison. The two men emerge from the subway

1.11 *Three Colours: White* (Krzysztof Kieślowski, 1994)

station, Karol pointing up in the direction of a Brigitte Bardot poster, for the film *Le Mépris* (*Contempt*). Both the film's title and Bardot's figure echo Dominique's flinty scorn and the appearance of the china bust. Bardot has the untouchable appeal of the film star (as, indeed, does Delpy). Displayed on the billboard in a state of undress, Bardot's image is at once erotically inviting and impenetrable, encased in a glossy plastic frame. Another frame draws Karol's attention though, just to the left. Behind drawn curtains and bathed in cream light, the black profile of Dominique takes a lover. Separated by curtains, the window, the apartment block, across the street, Dominique has become just as unreachable as Bardot's iconic image. The suggestion calcifies as Karol descends to call her from the subway phone. The phone booth forms a plastic sphere, half-white, half see-through. It encases Karol as he listens to Dominique's orgasmic moans. A close-shot holds Karol's face under the moulded surfaces. As Dominique cries out in pleasure, streaks of white light glint off the plastic. She wants him to hear her climax, down the phone. While she abandons herself to the noisy sex, Karol contains himself, struck dumb. The slashes of white light score the surface like signs of wounded pride. His wife's sexual and manipulative delight is transparent, taking Karol further from her even as, opaquely, such divisions will bring them closer.

1.12 *Three Colours: White* (Krzysztof Kieślowski, 1994)

Happy landings

Stifling his response to Dominique's infidelity, Karol finds release in another form of containment. He squashes himself into his battered brown suitcase, illicitly accompanying Mikolaj on his flight back home. The change of country offers a new outlook. In many ways, Poland presents Karol with the total whiteout necessary for his 'rebirth'. Far away from the subway's sickly fluorescent slick, snowy hills fill the frame. The snow presents a softer setting than previous white spaces: a much more malleable environment. As Karol makes his journey from France to Poland, *White* balances suggestions of weight and levity. The man-filled suitcase teeters on the top of a cartload of luggage. Then, the villainous airline workers who lug the case to a deserted spot, to share the spoils, are surprised when Karol bursts forth. He tumbles down the hill, careering out [see plate 4]. He makes a weighty landing in the snow: all the energies of his previous hard knocks now roll into his claim on the land. (His first and life-changing job in Poland will be as a *heavy*). Karol drops into the middle of a snowy nowhere; later, he buys up plots of seemingly worthless land. On a bright white map, his finger points out the red dot of his newly purchased farmhouse, now worth millions to the merciless property developers. Whereas the hairdressing diplomas roll away in the underground, these white plans are neatly laid. Sharing his newfound wealth with Mikolaj, Karol celebrates by skating on the surface of the city's iced lakes: no more frozen assets. Encased in the white cube of his office block, he becomes a hard-edged businessman (dealing, we learn, in white goods). Yet, despite seemingly having everything, the flurry of the world at his feet, Karol is still taunted by the china figure's luminous presence on the shelf. Watching a hefty sum of money mount up allows him to make a final defiant leap into nothingness.

Oblivion

To draw Dominique out of her impassive state and bring her close, Karol must erase himself completely, and pretend to die. It is more than fitting that this morbid hoax is presented in the blackest designs of the film. Mortality's shroud hangs lightly over *White*: in Mikolaj's bleak proposition, the performance of Karol shooting Mikolaj (a journey to the void stopped by him using blanks), and Karol's final revenge in faking his own death. Driven by the finality of Karol's apparent demise or the promise of plentiful inheritance, Dominique makes the trip from France to his funeral. From this moment on, officially 'dead', Karol works to control his chosen perspective of his wife. Previously, others position him, as when he stands opposite Dominique in the dock. Or else he is only present to her absence, for example, when she takes a lover in their apartment. Now he appears to determine the level of detachment. He spies on her as she cries over his casket. However, as her tears fall in a long-anticipated moment of emotional outpouring, a cut to black removes to a later place and time, when Dominique returns to her hotel room. Her silhouette forms in an unlit doorway. In the dimmed space, scant white light picks out silvery wisps of her blonde hair. At this stage, although a revelation is near, the film keeps her in the dark. While Karol believes he has the upper hand, it is an uncertain time. Their relationship is newly reshaping. The repeated sight of Dominique in the gloom cannot be Karol's view (he is waiting for her in the bed). While he may have more control, his vision of her remains indirect. As the couple draw closer together again, everything is up in the air. Haunting his own funeral, while Karol shadows his wife, Dominique's image appears unusually and obscurely insubstantial. For Karol, apparent assertions of control only serve to make things vague.

Consummation

The moment of physical reconciliation hardens Karol's resolve. Turning on the light, alive and well in Dominique's bed, he lays bare. Loose red sheets drape around soft pale skin. All containment is now gone, and his appeal is newly firm. Dominique crosses the room to the bed. The film cuts to close-up. Two pale hands reach to touch in front of drawn blue curtains [see plate 5]. Recalling the bold colour of other obstacles (the railings, the police van), the curtains form a fitting backdrop to the achievement of reunion. As the couple make love, the shots cut their bodies up into separate parts: a head, a hand, each as white as bone china. Severed from the whole by darkness, Karol's head now rests on Dominique's lap with the same heaviness previously felt in the carriage of the porcelain bust: a turnaround marking his self-posses-sion. Dominique reaches orgasm; the screen floods with pure white light. The film's decision to withhold a stylisation of whiteness until just this moment of absolute release is well-judged. As the couple finally consummate their fractured marriage, at the peak of their union, everything comes to an end. An ecstatic *petit mort* leads into an all-consuming emptiness. The effect is penetrating: now Karol can happily withdraw from Dominique's presence. After the sex, physi-cal hardness falls away while psychological resistance grows.

1.13 *Three Colours: White* (Krzysztof Kieślowski, 1994)

Karol quietly arranges loose strands of Dominique's hair as she sleeps. Crossing to the window, his hands and face touch against the curtains. Dominique stood alone in the wedding fantasia, teasingly separated by her drifting veil. Now Karol moves near to a white screen to close his scheme. This is the climax of his dreams. He leaves without a word.

A life untangled

Back in his brother's salon, with Dominique arrested under suspicion of his 'murder', Karol slowly passes his silver comb across his eyes. Looking through the comb gives him a slight layer of separation from the world. Across its hard teeth, things look a little different. Although the film does not cut to a point-of-view (POV) shot from Karol's perspective, one can imagine the effect would be similar to that of a flicker-book, or a strip of film spooling across shutters. As if conjuring a silver-screen fantasy, the wedding dream plays again, just for Karol. This time he is in the picture, kissing Dominique. Here, *White* suggests that, through the trials with his ex-wife, Karol embraces his own sense of separateness. He finds a solid form of disconnection, of disentanglement, leading to peaceful settlement. A closing emphasis on physical lines and barriers brings the suggestion to a head. We

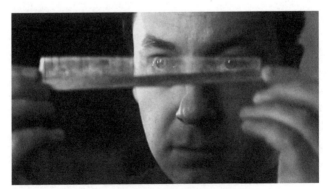

1.14 *Three Colours: White* (Krzysztof Kieślowski, 1994)

have reached the final sequence of the film. Karol goes to see Dominique in the prison. Solid white lines of paint stretch across the prison gates, a visual companion to the comb's upright teeth. Horizontal and vertical lines then combine in the steel mesh covering Dominique's cell window. As the camera draws near to witness her decisive opaque gesture, its move blurs and passes beyond the metal bars. On the point of connection, these barriers only seem to melt away. In the last shot of the film, lowering a pair of white binoculars, Karol no longer needs to shield his view of Dominique. He looks up to her directly and smiles. Crucially though, for the (ex) couple, the solid white bars are still there to stand between them. The lovers achieve reconciliation in mutual separation.

2 *Equinox Flower*
(Yasujiro Ozu: Japan, 1958)

'People who like red are either geniuses or madmen.'
(**Yasujiro Ozu**)[32]

Released in 1958, *Equinox Flower* brings to an end Ozu's long-standing resistance to the use of colour in film. Ozu's hesitation to embrace technological change compares with that of Charlie Chaplin, particularly in relation to *City Lights* (1931). Sceptical of the clamour for sound that appears to engulf classical Hollywood, Chaplin applies the element sparingly in *City Lights*, subtitling the film 'A Comedy Romance in Pantomime'. Throughout Chaplin's film, a small selection of aural effects appears at precise points. Each sound is measured and exact, crucial to the narrative and the development of meaning. Moreover, *City Lights* retains many of the stylistic characteristics of silent cinema, successfully integrating sparse sounds alongside established techniques.[33]

Like Chaplin and in the use of colour, Ozu applies spare and exacting tones and shades from a limited spectrum. Just as *City Lights* holds onto many aspects of silent cinema, monochrome pervades *Equinox Flower*. Throughout, black-and-white objects and images are organised into significant arrangements, crucial to the film's key dramatic points and expressive depth. Alongside monochromatic tones, a restricted selection of colours combines in delicate traces and dashes. Above all, as noted in the quotation that introduces this chapter, the film channels attention on small applications and various shades of the colour red.

The title of the film refers to the red higanbana flower that blooms during the autumn equinox in Japan. An equinox occurs when Sun and Earth come into alignment along the equator. Around equinox, nights and days are approximately equal in length. In Japan, the March Equinox Day is an official holiday, spent holding family reunions. In *Equinox Flower*, a father gradually, reluctantly warms to his young daughter's chosen suitor. Red adds a glowing blush to many frames in the film, often as a conduit between characters or other visual elements. Modern and traditional techniques form a union to match the marriage of young lovers and the consolidation of an older generation.

Ozu's tightly controlled application of colour is in keeping with his personal aesthetic. The moderation of the palette matches a restrained style of performance, and the limited movements of the camera. Occasional punctuations of red colouring correspond with the interspersion of 'still life' landscape shots. As well as being sparing in its application of red, *Equinox Flower* also moves the colour away from its more usual appearance in narrative film as a marker of dramatic hyperbole. As Laure Brost notes:

> Red has played a crucial and emphatic role since the beginning of colour film: red lanterns in a red light district, red smoke, red flowers, and entire sequences bathed in red ... one is struck by the vast and insistent varieties of red, for example, the boundless qualitative and quantitative ranges of blood, to say nothing of the arresting rubies, scarlets and other shades found in the great fabric waves of wardrobe and set design. Red eyes, red lips, and red shoes.[34]

In cinema aesthetics, red often becomes 'layered through figuration with emphasis and significance.'[35] Ozu's reds are bold but they only coat everyday items. Far from 'boundless qualitative and quantitative ranges of blood', *Equinox Flower* features red tea kettles, packets, radios, carpets, and flowers.

The choice of colour concentrates the items' presence and their aesthetic object. In their redness, the items both invite remark on their place in the film, and their place in the world. However, in camera placement and composition, the film does not push them to prominence (they are not 'emphatic', 'insistent' or 'arresting'). Rather, they contain and express the incidental energies found in many of our daily activities. This is a very different affective quality than that created in examples of red's hyperbole. To cite Brost again, 'Hyperbole demands that we ascend through a suprarordinary figuration articulated in style ... engaging in a language game that moves beyond ordinary articulation in order to express the full depth of a heightened and extreme circumstance.'[36] In contrast, dabs of red punctuate *Equinox Flower*'s story of ordinary life, quietly stimulating rather than thrillingly dramatic in their presence. For some scholars of Ozu, the director's distinct use of red leads to a different sort of 'language game'.

David Bordwell takes Ozu's handling of colour as part of a game with film form. Ozu's films make repeated uses of crosscutting and graphic matches: juxtaposing like images across different shots and spaces. This creates an 'abstract similarity among items.'[37] According to Bordwell, the repetition of such designs comprises 'visual puns', the point of which is 'for the viewer to create, on the fringe of the action, a zone of purely pictorial play.'[38] He provides an example from *Good Morning* (*Ohayô*, 1959) of, 'Crosscutting between locales,' as 'often governed by a more subtle comic innovation: a shot of one person, seated or standing, will give way to a similarly-scaled shot of another person, in the same posture but observed from another angle.'[39] The same occurs with the colour of certain objects, especially in red. Bordwell notes how (again in *Good Morning*), 'Ozu cuts from a washline to a living room; we cannot link the shots by inclusion and their spaces are only 'adjacent' in a loose sense; what links them are the red shirt in the upper right corner of shot 1 and the red lampshade in the same spot of shot 2.'[40] Turning to *Equinox Flower*, Bordwell emphasises his belief that these colour

effects are formal tricks or gags. He suggests that, 'Colour
film allows Ozu to highlight glasses and crockery in front of
the characters and to show every glass as containing liquid
at exactly the same level – as if more than a few viewers in
the world would catch the joke.'[41] Such shots may provide a
little twinkle of pleasure for the observant viewer. Yet, their
categorisation as 'purely pictorial play' takes something
richer away. They are more than parts of a formal game of
'Snap'. In Ozu's films, meaning gently accrues in instances
of repetition and resonance. As Andrew Klevan suggests of
Late Spring (Banshun, 1949):

> [T]he unique opportunities provided by film's narration
> through images allow for compositional patterning which can
> be developed over the course of the film. This stylistic capability
> constructed around repetition demonstrates that the medium
> is quite suited to uncovering insight in those elements of life
> which do not immediately proclaim their significance – for
> example, habitual behaviour around familiar spaces, small
> gestures, domestic furniture and empty rooms.[42]

In light of Klevan's work, this chapter on *Equinox Flower*
explores a kindred interest in 'habitual behaviour around
familiar spaces', and in patterns of repetition, particularly
around household objects. Klevan's account of a black-and-
white film necessarily leaves out thoughts on colour. My
reading of a later Ozu film places emphasis on the element's
introduction. While touches of colour may push our attention
towards certain designs a little more demonstrably than in
Late Spring, they do so in gentle appeals rather than forceful
orchestrations. Shades of colour adorn objects and characters
that are 'animated gradually by a developing significance'.[43]
The sight of similarly coloured objects juxtaposed in frames
and across shots form graphic resemblances. These are both
delightful and meaningful.

First signs

The credit sequence introduces the film's bearing towards colour, and hints at its overarching concerns. Characteristically for Ozu's works, the credits lack any showy embellishment. Black, white, and red Japanese writing appears on a tawny sea-grass background. The image opens up several of the film's central schemes. It observes a sparseness of palette, using a limited range of colours. It affirms that, despite the technological and stylistic possibilities now at its disposal, this film will concentrate on red and sustain an interest in the use of monochrome. In the meeting of black, white, and red symbols, the film sketches out its subsequent thematic interest in acts of coupling and contrast. The juxtaposition of different textures is also of note, as the natural coarse fibres of the background matting receive little coats of colour, glossy characters. Like the director, the fabric of the credit sequence takes on colour in a measured fashion. A modern synthetic treatment embosses traditional designs.

Three stark shots usher in the narrative: the front of a station building; railway lines and signal house; a close-up of a platform departure board. Such a locale usually fills with considerable hustle and bustle and we might expect to see this here. Instead, senses of stillness and emptiness mark out shots devoid of human business. The colour is mute and moderate: dusky-ochre and brown. The first, slight movement occurs as the counters on an opal-green departure board click and shuffle round, erasing the notice of a newly arrived train. In refraining from signs of motion until just this point and action, adding a touch more colour, the film notes significance in the lightest of strokes. It is an adjustment about making adjustments. (Railway boards appear at the beginning and end of the film, signals of interest. The final moments also show the central protagonist seated on a train, crossing tracks.)

The first human activity of the film brings new colours and signs of things to come. A cut moves out to the platform's edge, revealing a lively crowd of young people. Some

of the men wear black kimonos, while others are dressed in
black-and-white suits. Delicate prints of red flowers adorn
the women's matching white kimonos [see plate 6]. The
combination of colours recalls that of the credit sequence.
Here, the union of blacks, whites, and reds is in accord with
the coming together of couples: these are newlyweds greeting their partners. The red flower designs echo the film's title
(another marriage). A further cut reveals two platform attendants seated on a nearby bench, quietly watching the happy
throng. Dressed in matching black-and-white uniforms, they
offer their own lively commentaries on the proceedings, as a
humorous, makeshift Greek chorus:

> Guard 1: I guess this is a happy day.
> Guard 2: How so?
> Guard 1: Lots of newly-weds.
> Guard 2: Not a lot of pretty brides though.
> Guard 1: Did you see the one on the 15?
> Guard 2: The fat one? She's the prettiest so far.

The attendants cattily enact the issue of selection that will
occupy the film's central story: views on the choice of a suit-
able spouse. A close-up shot ends the sequence and caps the
suggestion. At the side of the platform, a little circular sign
announces, 'Warning: Strong Winds'. A black vertical stripe
marks a dash down a red and white background. The red
is the brightest shade yet, with its declarative tone matching that of the sign's message. It couples with the red of the
kimono flowers. Connections begin to form, of red, flowers,
marriage, storms. In a restrained use of colour and a gentle
prelude, the film forecasts the trouble ahead.

Black-and-white tradition ... to flushes of colour

Equinox Flower explores the connection between black-and-
white trappings and tradition. The next sequence observes
the ceremonies of a wedding banquet, to which, as close
friends of the bride, the Hirayama family is invited. In his
stiff white collar and plain black suit, Mr Hirayama (Shin

Saburi) appears as a standard-bearer of formality. Soon after the banquet, as he prepares for the more melancholy ceremony of a funeral, Mr Hirayama tells his wife that, again, 'a suit and black tie will do'. At home and his drinking club, he wears a black kimono with a white sash. Elsewhere, in a playful touch, as Mr Hirayama finds himself in the unfamiliar environs of a downtown bar, he perches stiffly in front of a sign advertising '"Black and White": Traditional Scotch Whisky'. Throughout the film, the use of monochrome links with this character's old-fashioned measures.

It is characteristic of Ozu's style that a seminal occasion such as a wedding becomes a ceremony pocketed within everyday routines. The film finds ways to celebrate the day as both special and as passing into the regular course of things. It primarily focuses on the guests, rather than the newlyweds. For the invitees, instead of a dramatic turning point, the day is a pleasing and brief suspension of life's regular rhythms. *Equinox Flower* encourages this understanding in the progression towards the banquet. The sound of a traditional wedding song bleeds from an external shot of the building and carries inside. The company moves through the hallway in the same style of passers-by in the subsequent scene, bustling outside a drinking club. The film directs a ceremonial procession towards more commonplace passages. Gliding in single file, the wedding guests step across a strip of deep red carpet: a habitual marker of special occasions [see plate 7]. The carpet sweeps vertically in the frame, through the centre of a grand hallway, prominent but necessarily passed over. The film later bridges the view with an equivalent shot, as the guests depart. (They walk back over the carpet right to left.) The crossing and re-crossing of the company over the red carpet act as punctuation marks, commas. The characters note suspensions in regular proceedings without stopping the line's flow.

Within the banqueting hall, the film presents the wedding as both celebratory and ceremoniously reserved. Colourful touches brush the set arrangements. The first view of the hall paints a picture of balance and proportion. Two rows of seated

guests point diagonally inwards towards the top table, left
and right. The top table sits horizontally, spanning the width
of the frame. The design emphasises not only the taut order
of the event, but also the marriage of two sides. Recognis-
ing the ceremonial constraints of the occasion, the company
is still, bowing their heads, listening to the wedding song.
The film brings sound and colour together in harmony. As if
absorbing the deep and rich tones of the song, dusky blocks
of maroon fill the high walls. Underneath, all fall under the
spell of the sound, cocooned in a private celebration. At the
centre of the quietly enchanted collective, colourful objects
near to the newlyweds add a whispering note of pleasure. A
few red flowers set by the happy couple peep out, letting a
little stirring of emotion into the austere procedures. As the
film moves closer to the newlyweds, a sense of stifled excitement gains fuller expression. Whilst the couple sit still and
silent, eyes turned to the laden table, their decorative trappings are at once declamatory and restrained. Arrangements
of red, pink, and yellow flowers form little tasteful displays
[see plate 8]. The flowers edge the frame: curbed stimulations
of colour. The gold spray of the bride's hairpins and the red
blush of her kimono put the final touches to a moment of
bright unspoken gladness.

The household objects

In repeated views of the Hirayama home, colours define
everyday patterns and adjustments, as well as letting impressions of the wedding linger. Brightly coloured domestic
objects gain resonance in their reappearance. The film again
uses red to mark them. A few simple items integrate easily
within the modest setting, at home. In their colouring, they
carry a quiet charge. The first views of the Hirayama household introduce objects in two rooms. A stout cast-iron kettle
sits in the foreground of the hallway, its bright red colour
adding a touch of warmth to the otherwise plain setting. In
the living room, a tabletop vase boasts a red and yellow floral

display. We will return to the kettle when the film does. First, there is a concentration of attention on the vase, and on the family's routes around it. The flowers recall those of the wedding bouquets. Just as the Hirayama family has returned with the bloom as a keepsake, the flowers bring home the idea of marriage.

The sequence turns on the family and flowers' bordering arrangements. Following the ceremony and after drinks at his club, Mr Hirayama heads home. On hearing the front door slide open, Mrs Hirayama (Kinuyo Tanaka) interrupts a chore to greet her husband. The camera traces her movement, crossing the floor and past the vase of flowers. The film joins Mrs Hirayama's bustle with that of her youngest daughter, Hisako (Miyuki Kuwano). The child dashes in the same direction from a different room. They move in unison. The image suggests how mother and daughter mirror each other's actions. It is also an observation of how the father's arrival causes the family to come to attention. Though they make different entrances, the women draw together by the vase of flowers. The bloom becomes a fulcrum to the family dynamic. In the father's appearance, the pattern subtly alters. In his moves through the living room, Mr Hirayama does not acknowledge the flowers' bright spray. He stands with his back to the vase, busying himself with practical matters: placing down his wallet, taking off his jacket and waistcoat. Even at home, although he removes items of formal attire, the character makes everyday rituals a priority. The ignored flowers infuse the atmosphere. Conversation turns to the subject of eldest daughter Setsuko (Ineko Arima) and her courtship. Their words draw them closer to the bouquet. As if summoned by the discussion, Setsuko comes home. On entering the living room, she makes a beeline for the flowers, bending down to smell them. Embracing the bouquet, it is Setsuko who now gathers the family's attention, facing rather than circling a thorny issue.

As punctuations of daily activities, two unexpected arrivals to the Hirayama household are most revelatory. They bring

2.1 *Equinox Flower* (Yasujiro Ozu, 1958)

to light the film's use of colour to mark subtle and swift shifts
in mood. Fleeting visits modify established patterns of behaviour, colour them differently. Coming to the Hirayama home,
a daughter and mother make separate calls and impressions.
First, Yukiko Sasaki (Fujiko Yamamo) appears unannounced,

2.2 *Equinox Flower* (Yasujiro Ozu, 1958)

finding Mr Hirayama home alone. Later, her mother – 'Mrs. Sasaki of Kyoto' (Chieko Naniwa) – makes a similar journey, encountering Mrs Hirayama, again without the family. The film is playfully instructive of the two visits' similarities and differences. It encourages parallels by marking them out in a matching order and framing of shots. (There are, after all, family resemblances.) At the same time, differing combinations of colour express opposing effects. In the first visit, Yukiko brightens Mr Hirayama's humour and breathes new life into the home. In the second, Mrs Sasaki succeeds only in unsettling the atmosphere.

The first is a meeting of different generations. Lively colours and conversation loosen Mr Hirayama's guard. Yukiko's visit moves the narrative away from the stuffy confines of Hirayama's office, and adds breeziness inside the family home. The sequence opens in the street: sun-dappled and drowsy. The young girl's arrival wakens the setting. A shiny teal taxi draws into the street [see plate 9]. The colour of the car brings out the greens of the trees lining the street: new meets old. It also hints at Yukiko's youthful influence, stimulating but still green. On the soundtrack, a harp announces the taxi's arrival at the home. As if cued by the melody, the driver steps out to open the passenger door. His standard-issue black-and-white outfit brings to mind that of the train guards and the formal suits of the male wedding guests. Yukiko answers a question from the driver with a cursory instruction ('should I wait?' 'No, you can leave'). She approaches the house. The Hirayamas' elderly housemaid appears at the door, also in a black-and-white uniform, bowing (as is custom). Even before meeting with her friend's father, the young girl is at ease with traditionally prescribed roles, and good at directing them.

In reds, the sequence explores the notion of 'making oneself at home'. The ruby sash of Yukiko's kimono couples with the red stripes of a gift-wrapped box, held ready for presentation. Both connect with the red of the kettle, set squat on the floor. The link of particular objects, of gift and kettle, hints at a wish for modest celebration, of reward and refreshment. As Mr Hirayama guides his guest into his home, each move reveals further measures of happy accommodation. Opening an inner door, the host decides against a first space ('you'll like the other room better'). Adjustments are made to please. As the characters move into the heart of the home, reds collect to suggest Yukiko making her own adaptations. Like the composition of the doorway greeting, red objects in the living room link together by their presence. Here they do so along a loose horizontal line: a radio perched on a shelf, the gift-wrapped box, the teakettle. Taking central position in the frame, Yukiko kneels to complete the pattern, her red kimono sash set by the table [see plate 10]. With poise, the film suggests the effects of Yukiko's appearance. The young girl doesn't stand out or entirely blend in with the wider environs of this home. Instead, she is in line with its sites of gentle diversion: the radio, the gift, the kettle. She draws out the small measures of warmth that are already there.

Such charming calculations develop into a little enchantment. Gradually, Hirayama falls under Yukiko's spell. As they chat, Yukiko drifts from room to room. A gentle turn away from camera and host reveals that her sash collects as a larger ruby crest on the back of the kimono. In the young girl's moves through the house, the bright crest infuses each still, empty room. The permeation of red hints at how Yukiko's youthful vitality is beginning to colour Hirayama's more usually black-and-white mindset. In opposition to his subsequent and strongly held views on his daughter's position, he suggests to Yukiko that 'A pretty girl like you shouldn't hurry to marry brass.' Ultimately, Yukiko will manage to get Hirayama to agree to his daughter marrying an 'unsuitable' suitor. The playful adjustments of this initial visit filter into a later, bolder set-up.

Whereas Yukiko's visit marks a display of careful balancing, pleasantly calculated to warm up Mr Hirayama, her mother proves a less complementary guest. Mrs Sasaki's tattling manner creates a sense of discordance. Her presence niggles rather than nurtures. Initially, the arrival of the mother appears to rhyme fully with that of the daughter. The second visit begins with a matching long shot of the street; the taxi follows the same route as the earlier car; the driver is dismissed with the same words. In this scene though, a mother's company displaces the earlier brightness of youth. Rather than a shiny green car, Mrs Sasaki arrives in a pale yellow vehicle. The colour is appropriate for the carriage of this sickly woman, returning from a recent hospital visit. She may be ill, but like the colour, Mrs Sasaki has a tendency to overpower.

The older woman's designs are different from those of her daughter. Like Yukiko, she wears a green kimono, but this one is a touch duller. As Mrs Hirayama bustles to greet her surprise visitor, we see she too is similarly dressed. The matching colours may appear to hint at the mothers' kindred spirits, but Mrs Sasaki's pattern is more involved (perhaps a little *too* busy). Both mother and daughter bear gifts. This time, a pale green box replaces the more inviting red bundle. There is no sign of the red teakettle. As the two mothers move into the living room, there is the provision of tea, but it is

2.3 *Equinox Flower* (Yasujiro Ozu, 1958)

not from the red kettle or a shared activity. As Mrs Hirayama excuses herself for a moment, the maid hurriedly delivers the visitor a single blue cup. In place of the earlier visit's warm embrace of reds, the blue cup hints at a cooler atmosphere. There is a more particular suggestion too, as Mrs Sasaki later complains of how the doctor in the sanatorium 'injected [her] with some kind of blue ink. It turned everything blue.' Rather than a gentle infusion, taking tea with Mrs Sasaki is a bitter pill.

Instead of suggesting Yukiko's playful and precise manipulations, here the blocking of colours and space matches Mrs Sasaki's obstructive behaviour. In the living room, directly behind the space occupied by Yukiko as she knelt to present her little red gift, two bright red socks dangle from a drying rack, as if traces of the previous moment. As Mrs Sasaki stoops to kneel in the same spot, her body obscures the socks, covering up a suggestion of earlier warmth. Equally, in movements through the house, the mother's bustle takes the place of Yukiko's delicate manoeuvres. Reluctantly, Mrs Hirayama agrees to help determine their daughters' suitors. With characteristic abruptness, Mrs Sasaki interrupts her, announcing a necessary trip to use the bathroom. She sets off in the wrong direction. Her hasty movements are misguided. She bumbles from room to room, a pale imitation of Yukiko's magical glow.

Mrs Sasaki's troublesome visit concludes with an odd gesture and tinge of colour. Rushing through the hallway, the guest suddenly pauses to hang a broom by its peg on a hook, on the wall. Aquamarine light glows from the bathroom [see plate 11]. Having performed her little act of putting things right, she withdraws out of the frame. The luminous blue air spreads awkwardly into the natural browns and greens of the house, as out of place as the unwanted visitor. The tint also recalls her sanatorium tale, of being 'injected with some kind of blue ink.' The character carries a clinical air into the Hirayama house, and in her planning for the daughters' futures. Both the blue light and a mother's meddling are unpleasantly artificial contrivances. She places the broom on the wall, determined to set things in order. Yet, her involvement in arrangements leads only to disturbance. As Mrs Sasaki moves away to relieve herself, the broom swings gently back and forth: a passing agitation.

Acts of union

As Mr Hirayama relaxes his stance on his daughter's romantic wishes, the film releases more colour. The naughty interventions of Yukiko and the experience of seeing a friend's daughter (Fumiko [Yoshiko Kuga]) in love with her 'unsuitable suitor' change Mr Hirayama's attitude. It happens gradually, in step with new inflections of colour in established settings: the dining table, the golf club, the male domain of the sake bar. The young people's happy union stimulates these rigidly prescribed 'black-and-white' worlds.

Before Mr Hirayama gives his consent for Setsuko's marriage, his wife is more flexible. In a view seen before in the film, man, wife, and daughter sit at the dining table. An argument about Setsuko's lover flares up. The young girl flees in tears. When Mr Hirayama plainly restates his position, his wife risks a new outlook: 'But, Taniguchi looks like a good man.' As her words take flight, piquing her husband, Mrs Hirayama fidgets in front of a bright frieze of soaring birds. The birds are coloured peach and pink in a lime-green sky. In a pastel flutter and a quiver of excitement, film and character allow a fanciful vision to form.

The possibility of consent also colours daily life in more unspoken ways. In the last view of the Hirayama living room, the red teakettle takes centre stage. A nearby cup suggests the kettle's use. Likewise, the red radio fulfils its purpose. As Mrs Hirayama again busies herself, awaiting her husband's return, the sound of traditional song fills the room. Although, on entering, Mr Hirayama demands that his wife turn off the music, something is in the air. As Mrs Hirayama smiles to herself, we again find her company in the frieze of painted

birds. With music and the return sight of the pastel picture,
the mood lifts a little more.

Finally, film and father broaden their outlooks together. In
the concluding scenes, *Equinox Flower* opens out the setting,
moving from the confines of the home to the wider vistas
of a golf club. In this exclusive, notoriously regimented
setting, men gather to test their form. (There are no women
on this course.) On the green of the golf course, although
the black-and-white uniform of the business suit gives way
to beige and brown slacks, rigid systems of conduct are still
in place. Protocol dictates the order of play. For Mr Hirayama
though, private contemplations of the wedding shade into his
game. The golf flags, painted in red and yellow stripes, bear
the film's colours of marriage. (*Equinox Flower* has fun by
marrying associations on the links, playing a formal game.)
More matches occur in the clubhouse. Heavy brown furniture and dark red matting recall the colours of the earlier
wedding venue. As camera and protagonist move to the bar,
yellow ashtrays and pink barstools evoke the garish palette
of the Luna bar, Fumiko's place of work. The father of the
bride at the earlier wedding – Mr Kawai (Nobuo Nakamura)
– suddenly appears, relating news of Mrs Hirayama's request
that he take the role of intermediary at Setsuko's wedding.
On the golf course and in the club, even when trying to 'get
away from it all', Mr Hirayama finds himself in another position of necessary adjustments. A sense of consolidation gathers pace.

Rather than show the wedding itself, the film filters the
event through two final reunions. The two acts confirm a
further, more fragile alliance, between father and daughter.
One gathering takes place before Setsuko's wedding ceremony, in the Hirayama home. One comes after, at the fathers'
school reunion. On the eve of the wedding, a celebration meal
transforms the family dining table. The red teakettle sits
close by. A red patterned cloth lies over a table festooned with
orange pop bottles and glasses of red wine, other reminders
of the wedding ceremony that opened the film. Apparently

2.4 *Equinox Flower* (Yasujiro Ozu, 1958)

still reluctant to agree to Setsuko's wishes, Mr Hirayama
retreats to his bedroom. Finally, he grants permission in the
guise of a token handed to his wife: two white gloves and a
black tie. It is especially fitting that a restrained willingness
to consent is measured in these prim items of formal attire.
There is a further, funny consolation in colours. Returning to the living room, Mr Hirayama stoops to sit, resting
his hands on the brightly decorated table. Having given in,
given his consent, the father finds support in his family's
communal demonstration. The bright red and orange table-
ware amplifies good cheer, like giddy Christmas revellers (or
rowdy wedding guests).

As a companion piece, the fathers' reunion marks a more
soulful consolidation of new and old in song. The wedding
takes place, but the focus stays with the fathers. A close circle
of old school-friends gathers, cocooned in the sanctuary of a
sake bar. Lit by the moon, the reunion eclipses the wedding's
unseen festivities. This magical space grants each man time
to reflect on events past and present, on the transformation
of their daughters into women and wives. All the men wear
matching black-and-white striped gowns, with dark red sake

bottles and rice bowls at hand [see plate 12]. For the last time, the film couples monochrome and crimson, allowing for a final celebratory union. While the men are resplendent in their traditional robes, defiantly singing 'out of date' laments, they raise a glass to their children's futures.

3 *The Green Ray*
(Eric Rohmer: France, 1986)

'The day was very clear and dry; there were no clouds.
He said, "Maybe we'll be lucky today," and I did see it,
Just for a second, when the sun set on the horizon,
At the final stage, there was a kind of pale green shaft,
Like a sword blade, a horizontal beam,
Very pretty, but extremely brief.

When you see the green ray,
You can read your feelings and others' too.'
(**Elderly man**, *The Green Ray*)

A natural artistry

The above words are spoken by one of a gathering of bit-part players in *The Green Ray*. The lines point towards certain ways of seeing: being lucky enough to see a pure green ray of light when the sun meets the sea at a particular point and time; reading your feelings clearly when the ray appears; seeing something familiar (the sun, the horizon, yourself, others) from a new perspective, as remarkable. In discussing their personal experience of the green ray, the characters cast a fictional tale (Jules Verne's 1882 novel *The Green Ray*) into a happening from their own lives. The words are a good place to start, not only in opening up concerns of colour in the film to hand, but also as introducing thoughts of Eric Rohmer's particular style of filmmaking.

The natural artistry of the green ray's appearance transforms the everyday scenario of a sunset from within. It is a
perfect combination of unforced theatricality and reality, in
which the landscape quickly and quietly announces itself to
us, reminding us of the beauty inherent in the most habitual
of world views. We may not watch the sun setting every day,
but it sets. (Look at what we are missing, at what happens
when we stop to look, when an aspect of daily routine
changes). A small adaptation makes something normal
profound. When the lines of dialogue are set out as they are at
the start of this chapter, a natural poetry emerges from ordinary conversation. And, when Rohmer's camera is held on
the world, a world in which everyday scenarios are delicately
rearranged into fiction, a subtle visual poetry meets that of
the words. Such a responsive rendering of the world lies at
the heart of Rohmer's art, and of *The Green Ray*. Rather than
enforce cinema's stylistic features to create a melodramatic
distortion of reality, Rohmer achieves a sensitive balance of
art, artificiality, and naturalism. As Derek Schilling notes,
such measures reveal 'the filmmaker's power to reproduce
the unadorned beauty of things.'[44]

Similarly to *Three Colours: White* and *Equinox Flower*, one
particular colour is prominent in *The Green Ray*. As the film's
title suggests, shades of green comprise not only the 'story
within a story' – Jules Verne's tale within Rohmer's – but
also the key colour motif. Contained by green traces, yellows,
reds, and powder-blues develop the film's light palette.
Returning us to Turner's thoughts on 'the interiority of the
unknown woman in film', the colour arrangements often
express Delphine's private responses to the world around
her: external evocations of a particular state of mind.[45] In
particular, in its handling of pale colours, the film explores
aspects of irresolution.

The Green Ray focuses on the different experiences that
shade into one another during one summer's hazy plans.
It offers a meditation on holidaying, on the way relaxation
sometimes requires a willing commitment to the act (such

as is expressed in everyday remarks like, 'I can't wait for my vacation. I'm planning on doing absolutely nothing'). Throughout, the film explores Delphine's uncertain attempts at 'being on holiday'. Over the months of July and August, she is constantly in transit, held in between holiday destinations. The young Parisienne embarks on a series of cancelled trips across France, only to return time after time to the capital. She is never 'on vacation', always on and in retreat. In meetings with friends, family, and strangers, she flirts with relaxation, but keeps things bottled up. She never quite finds the space to express herself, to lay claim to a moment of leisure. Rather than frustration, the light colours of the film most often convey a sense of indeterminacy. A range of delicate shades expresses feelings that drift, decisions held in suspension, and a dilution of emotional clarity (the 'ability to read your feelings, and others' too').

On the periphery

Greenery brushes the first shot's borders. Just as one might catch sight of the green ray out of the corner of the eye, green objects appear in the margins of the film's compositions. A stone-faced office block looms under a slate-grey sky. Traces of greenery brighten and soften the building's hard edges. On the left, treetops swirl in leafy sprays. On the right, a forest-green canopy billows from a high window [see plate 13]. Seductively indirect traces of green tease our attention. The light animation of swaying branches and a fluttering canopy entice the eye away from blander, weightier matters of everyday business, distracting from the concrete. The colours inside the office turn the inference away from agitation to accommodation. Two female receptionists sit at cluttered desks. Gauzy curtains allow pale grey light to filter through open windows, fitting the humdrum mood yet suggesting a sense of airiness. The receptionists chatter in soft voices, breezy in their business. Lightness carries in their clothing. On the left, a pale blue blouse matches the shade of an adja-

cent typewriter. On the right, a pastel pink cardigan complements a portfolio close to hand.

Delphine's first appearance delicately introduces a more
complicated story. As the telephone rings, the reception-
ist beckons her in to take the call. Delphine enters centre
frame. Her outfit suggests that unlike her co-workers, she
fits slightly awkwardly here. A pale grey top complements
the shade of the telephone. Her skirt is the same pastel blue
as a neighbouring girl's blouse. Its flowery pattern includes a
similar pink to the other girl's cardigan. While Delphine's pale
colours harmonise with those of her co-workers, the skirt's
busy design stands out against the other clothes' singular
shades [see plate 14]. The muted grey jumper contrasts with
the skirt's pastel motif. When put upon, Delphine wavers
between fitting in and standing out. Her movements develop
this idea. She flits into and out of the frame, on the periphery.
As Delphine answers the call – an unexpected cancellation
of her holiday plans, one of many to come – she stands in
front of a sea-green angle lamp, craning into the frame. At
this moment, with all plans broken, the green ray remains
beyond her.

Pastel touches

Even at home, Delphine struggles to settle. It is now Friday,
the eighth of July. Delphine's holiday plans are still on hold.
On a hot summer's afternoon, she is stuck inside, nowhere
to go. Rumpled pink sheets tell of an earlier restless doze.
A discarded blouse sprawls upon the bed, as if wilting in
the heat [see plate 15]. A lone plant sits on a white dresser.
It stands in relief to the pale fabrics, its olive spray calling to
mind the promise of the green ray. Yet, it too seems rather
tired, its long fronds limply curling and drooping down.

The phone rings, breaking the heavy air. The film reframes.
Upright bottles and strips of streamers stretch in tight vertical
lines. The call enlivens the atmosphere. Character and décor
come to attention. Just as quickly though, indecision replaces

3.1 *The Green Ray* (Eric Rohmer, 1986)

a quick spurt of energy. Delphine hovers on the threshold of the balcony, half inside, and half out. Deciding to take the call, she stoops to cradle the receiver. As she speaks, there are gentle movements in the frame. A flamingo-pink fan flutters on the wall. A rosy towel swings in the breeze. Plump green

3.2 *The Green Ray* (Eric Rohmer, 1986)

plant leaves bob, touching her shoulder (almost). She tries to persuade a friend, Jean-Pierre, to accompany her to Antibes. In turn, the friend presses for other plans, leaning towards an alternative destination. Toying with the invitation, leaving it unanswered, Delphine lightly strokes her legs. The call allows ideas of holiday plans to drift, but decisions are better brushed away.

Uncharacteristic boldness

Occasionally, bolder colours appear in brief and rare instances of assertion. A first example picks up the film's interest in transitory moments and spaces, in the crossing of a street. The scene punctuates two uncertain responses to holiday invitations, of Delphine talking with her sister (as noted in the introduction), and the phone call from Jean-Pierre. In the street, Delphine passes a bright green lamp-post. With its strong colour and upright position, the post forms a bold punctuation, like an exclamation mark at the end of a sentence! It points the way to a surprising discovery. Walking by the post, Delphine is drawn to a little sea-green object on the pavement. Lying face down, a playing card boasts an insignia of golden horns of plenty. The image and instance rhyme with Delphine's later sighting of a deep green poster stuck to a lamp-post, boldly inviting the reader to 'regain contact with yourself and others'. Both imply finds of fortune, or fortunate finds, promising better things just over the horizon: little green rays of hope. In both instances, the film makes the uncharacteristic decision to cut to the card and poster in extreme close-up [see plates 16 and 17]. The central musical theme's atonal chords jar like the shots. Bold colours are presented as, and in, declamatory gestures. Whereas in a lesser film these techniques may be used crudely to draw attention to 'significant moments' (emphasised as dramatically pivotal), here they match Delphine's awkwardly intense experience of assertion. The green signs make brash claims on her attention, demanding concentration(s). Both card and the flyer are similarly blatant in their symbolic appeals. As such, although chance finds, they assert themselves too readily. Their connection to meaning is too easy to make. For Delphine, emotional clarity comes from indirect persuasions.

In instances when Delphine feels compelled to join in, loud colours express similarly awkward senses of contrivance. Rather than allowing measures of self-assurance to come out naturally, Delphine is forced (she forces herself) into artificial displays. A trapped emotional articulacy presses into flushes of boldness that only serve to set her further apart. An example occurs at a get-together with another friend, Manuela (María Luisa García), in a museum's grounds. A leisurely mood initially glosses the setting. A smooth green lawn and blossoming pink flowerbed bound the building. The shot provides a gentle reminder that the green ray borders each place visited by Delphine, just out of reach. Hazy sunshine turns arches and edges a light shade of peach. The diffused sunlight tones down the appearance of the stone, softening granite-grey surfaces. Similarly, the grounds' visitors find ways to make themselves comfortable here. A first quick shot

3.3 *The Green Ray* (Eric Rohmer, 1986)

shows Manuela perching to read on an outer wall ledge. In
second and third views, girls stretch out across low divides.
Two more shots present three people on green iron benches,
leaning back or forward, at rest. All of these people easily
adapt to this space's accommodations, relaxing into (the)
place.

Framed alone, Delphine stands at the gateway, half in, half
out of the grounds. The gate's heavy vertical slats and struts
contrast with the sloping couplings of bodies and walls. As
Delphine moves inside the grounds, the rusty gate squeaks
opens and closes with a rattle. She is wearing a bright red
jacket. For this character, reds express a complicated relationship to confidence. The coat's red is the boldest colour
Delphine will put on in the film. Like the gate, it grates. The
thick cut of the coat appears inappropriate for the muggy
summer weather. Boldness wears itself as a burden. In later
moments, on returning to Paris after an unsuccessful trip to
the mountains, Delphine ties a red cardigan tightly round
her waist. As she walks along the edge of the Seine, others
lie stripped to sunbathe. At her lowest point, Delphine treads
despairingly down to the water's edge on a lonely holiday in
Biarritz, wrapped in a red plastic windbreaker. The colour
and cloth hang heavily on the character, as (and at) points of
stress.[46]

Rather than fall in with the rest, Delphine stands awkwardly
alone. She is unable to appreciate the spell at the museum as
a little relaxing break. For her, it must be a means to an end,
to arranging a 'proper' holiday. Tellingly, her first words to
Manuela mark a desire to move on: 'Can we go elsewhere? It
hurts my eyes here. Sorry, but let's move into the shade.' The
chosen site fits her edgy disposition. She sits on the corner
of a wall, on the borderline of sun and shade, in between
two stone statues [see plate 18]. Throughout the scene, her
red coat marks her out amongst the breezy whites and softer
pastels. The colour emphasises not only Delphine's isolation
in this setting, but also her inability to find a holiday companion of similarly forthright designs. She cannot explain what

she wants, so is caught between plans. In attempting to express her situation with Manuela, Delphine lastly flushes with frustration. An attempt at emboldened confidence gives way to a flare of anxiety.

Strains of colour

Bold and pastel colours clash in moments of close physical gathering, especially around dinner tables. Delphine finds herself part of many such meetings, before and during the various interrupted holidays. The protagonist's contributions to mealtime conversations come out awkwardly. A good example of conflicting colours and temperaments occurs in a rendezvous of Delphine and friends in Paris. The ill-fated gathering comes moments after Delphine finds the green flyer, inviting her to 'rediscover contact with others'. The hackneyed promise leads instead to a quarrelsome lunch. A barrage of direct questions embarrasses Delphine. The group pressures her to holiday alone. Across the table, in tone, different colours accompany notes of stress and uncomfortable quietness.

The conversation between friends strays from pleasantries into intimate opinions. In the grey afternoon light, the camera focuses on each person in turn. In the first close shot, as tempers start to fray, Manuela, dressed in a black top, pats a black cat. A stroke of monochrome suggests an urge to stay neutral, yet the cat's wriggling adds a note of restlessness. Although Manuela may have something to say, she rubs away the urge to say it. Another's voice leads the discussion. Her name is Béatrice (Béatrice Romand). It is telling that Béatrice is the only person addressed by name in the scene, a little sign of her assertive personality. She chatters throughout, with gradually increasing urgency and aggression. The choice of a bright red blouson fits her well. Whereas the film dresses Delphine in red to express awkward attempts at being bold, here the emphasis is on a confident commitment to being loud [see plate 19]. Alongside the colour of the clothing, frills

and heavy rouge make-up accentuate the character's brashness. Goading Delphine to make her mind up and take a holiday, Béatrice overdoes it.

As well as reds, pastels look strained on another girl. When
Delphine appears in or close to pastels, like in the bedroom
scene, the colours accompany instances of listlessness and
indecision. In contrast, on the clothing of a different person
around the table, a busy collection of similarly pale shades
suggests a more emphatic unwillingness to concentrate. The
camera moves to the far right of the table, revealing a girl in a
fizz of pastel clothing [see plate 20]. She is wearing a pepper-
mint blouse and headband, and a candy-stripe necklace of
plastic baubles. The spray of babyish colours is an open declaration of giddiness. (Like a badge or car-bumper sticker, the
outfit is a forced display of personality). The girl chooses not
to join in the conversation, preferring just to titter. Her act as
pastel-painted ingénue is a little weak, and annoying. Amidst
these more gregarious tones, Delphine sits mute, dressed in
white. She listens quietly to the hot-headed suggestions and
giddy laughter, adding the odd remark. Although she appears
quite calm, a background colour hints at underlying agitation. A bright yellow towel hangs on a line behind Delphine's
head. As Béatrice's commentary becomes increasingly vigor-
ous, the wind blows the colourful fabric about, quietly worry-
ing.

A change in the light (from red to green)

The film finally releases a glimmer of hope, held in a glimpse
of the green ray. It is Saturday, the fourth of August. Delphine
has reached the end of her two-month vacation from work
without successfully completing a single holiday. A repeated
return home to Paris is the only act met with determination. Similarly, here, resolution in retreat carries in a burst
of colour. Preparing to leave her Biarritz cottage, Delphine
sits on the bed, phoning a taxi to take her away. The scene
and room are awash with shades of red: of Delphine's jacket,

3.4 *The Green Ray* (Eric Rohmer, 1986)

bedspread, on a nightlight, in sheets of wallpaper. The deep concentration of one colour emphasises the singular fixity of Delphine's mind, whilst the redness aggravates – she must flee now. She is too late. The train has gone. In the railway terminal, for the first time, Delphine has to submit to a passage of waiting. She accepts the pause in plans and settles into the spell. Carrying her heavy red baggage, she loosens the straps, and finally sits still.

Indirectly, far from the green poster's earlier assertion and false promises, the short wait gently lifts Delphine into a state of clarity. The intermediate space of a railway waiting room acts as a perfect go-between, opening her eyes to the surrounding possibilities (to the 'unadorned beauty of things'). From nowhere, a handsome young man appears, his entrance wittily accompanied by the rushing roll of a train's arrival. A play of glances ensues, eye contact at first avoided. Having rebuffed several forward men during her holidays, this man's incidental presence offers Delphine a roundabout way of approaching emotional candour. She introduces herself, and they leave the station to wait out in the open. By chance, Delphine spots the name of a roadside shop:

The Green Ray. Illumination ultimately comes in the most
cursory of settings. The film develops the brushing of green
borders: hilltop tufts appear on the horizon. Whilst fitting
with previous glimpses of green bushes, trees, canopies, and
fences, now Delphine picks out the cliff top: her attention is
at last directed, and direct. Her words to the man flow freely,
and are uncharacteristically frank. She goes further, deciding
that she will walk with him to the cliff top (at last deciding
on a destination). The twosome settle to watch the sun dip
down over the sea. All of a sudden, the green ray's flickering
appearance rewards their attention [see plate 21]. A little gasp
of laughter greets its arrival, Delphine's only one in the film.
It comes out naturally, unexpectedly. Her ripple of delight
meets with the swelling waves, and the refracting light of the
green ray: a moment of release, heralding the future's new
irresolution.

4 *Written on the Wind* (Douglas Sirk: US, 1956)

'Once upon a time there was a poor little rich boy who pickled his tiny brain with gin and bourbon, until he got so stinking blind he couldn't see what was going on under his big red nose.'
(**Marylee Hadley** (**Dorothy Malone**) to **Kyle Hadley** (**Robert Stack**), *Written on the Wind*)

An oil tycoon called Kyle Hadley, drunk on easy success and cheap liquor, falls into a dark and delirious fairytale of his own making. The colour scheme adopted to express this feverish rhapsody of wish and regret is as rich as the Hadley family. Intense colours swirl and spike in a kaleidoscope of intricate patterns. To achieve this effect, the film employs Technicolor®. The Technicolor system allows for rich saturations and brilliant arrangements.[47] For certain Golden Age Hollywood directors such as Vincente Minnelli and Douglas Sirk, the luminous spectrum of Technicolor complements their elaborate style. As Scott Higgins suggests, 'Watching a Technicolor film from the classical era is a perceptual luxury. We are impressed with the abundance of colour; and we sense that it has been carefully organised, shaped into compositions that feel complete, polished, and dramatically nuanced.'[48] *Written on the Wind* – a story of and about luxurious abundance – is an excellent example of this aesthetic relationship.

To understand the part played by Technicolor in the film, it is helpful here to note the relationship between melodrama and mise-en-scène. John Gibbs offers an eloquent account of Thomas Elsaesser's pioneering *Monogram* article 'Tales of Sound and Fury', addressing the complex handling of colour and widescreen in the domestic melodramas of the 1950s and 1960s (of which *Written on the Wind* is a celebrated example):

> Both physical and psychical characteristics of the genre, [Elsaesser] argues, make it particularly amenable to mise-en-scène … not only does the domestic setting provide an enormous range of plastic and spatial opportunities for filmmakers to create suggestive mise-en-scène, but also, in contrast to what Elsaesser calls the 'action genres' – musicals or westerns, for instance – the characters of domestic melodramas have no outlet for their emotions. In the action genres, such conflicts can be successfully 'externalised and projected into direct action', but in the melodramas the physical and social sphere in which the characters live means that they cannot openly express themselves or resolve concerns through dance or decisive action. As a result, Elsaesser argues, we witness 'a sublimation of dramatic conflict into decor, colour, gesture and composition of the frame, which in the best melodramas is perfectly thematised in terms of the characters' emotional and psychological predicaments.'[49]

In *Written on the Wind*, colour is 'perfectly thematised' as representative of both the characters' largesse, and their 'emotional and psychological predicaments.' That is to say, within an environment of dramatic amplification, insistent arrangements of colour convey a tendency for overbearing displays. At the same time, around assertive statements, the film's compositions carry subtle appeals. Showy colours match aspects of the characters' declamatory presence, but also prickle with subliminal energies.

As part of a carefully organised aesthetic, the use of Technicolor comes with the notoriously stringent regulations enforced on every production bearing that company's mark. One figure came to embody Technicolor's presence in and around the associated films: Natalie M. Kalmus. As Dalle Vacche and Price note:

Until Technicolor was deemed a monopoly, Kalmus served as an advisor on every film that chose to use Technicolor equipment. Her presence as advisor was a condition to which every producer seeking to use Technicolor had to agree. Kalmus's job was to provide the director with colour schemes appropriate to the narrative … [her essay] 'Color Consciousness' is an elaboration of Kalmus's aesthetic and is nothing less than a blueprint for understanding colour patterns and associations intended in Technicolor films. One could say without risk of overstatement that Kalmus was a genuine auteur, a figure whose signature is as evident, if not more so, as the more celebrated directors with whom she worked.[50]

Although *Written on the Wind* appears after Kalmus' reign at Technicolor (1934–49), it follows her blueprint under the watchful eye of the colour consultant on set, William Fritzsche. The role of the Technicolor consultant is to authorise all decisions made on colour coding and application. As Kalmus notes, 'In the preparation of a picture we read the script and prepare a colour chart for the entire production, each scene, each sequence, set and character being considered. This chart may be compared to a musical score, and amplifies the picture in a similar manner.'[51] Further, 'Color Consciousness' details a rigorous, all-embracing approach to specific colours. Let us consider Kalmus' (extensive) thoughts on red:

As to the use of a single color alone, each hue has its particular associations. For example, red recalls to mind a feeling of danger, a warning. It also suggests blood, life, and love. It is materialistic, stimulating. It suffuses the face of anger, it led the Roman soldiers into battle. Different shades of red can suggest various stages of life, such as love, happiness, physical strength, wine, passion, power, excitement, anger, turmoil, tragedy, cruelty, revenge, war, sin, and shame. These are all different, yet in certain respects they are the same. Red may be the color of the revolutionist's flag, and streets may run red with the blood of rioters, yet red may be used in a church ritual for Pentecost as a symbol of sacrifice. Whether blood is spilled upon the battlefield in an approved cause or whether it drips from the assassin's dagger, blood still runs red. The introduction of another color with red can suggest the motive for a crime whether it be jealousy, fanaticism, revenge, patriotism, or religious sacrifice. Love gently warms the blood. The delicacy or strength of red will suggest the type of love. By introducing the colors of licentiousness, deceit, selfish ambition, or passion, it will be possible to classify the types of love portrayed with considerable accuracy.[52]

This account is as lyrical and meticulously specific as it is exhaustive and exhausting. And, there's the rub. It is undeniably thoughtful in its firm associations of red with particular feelings, meanings, objects, and actions. At the same time, dependent on content and context, the list suggests that red can apply to anything and everything. Thus, whilst seemingly restrictive in its taut codification of colours in a film, Kalmus' compendious blueprint also infers that intuition (under agreement) dictates each specific application. Like many other directors, Douglas Sirk may have danced with Technicolor/Kalmus on certain decisions. Film historians have charted this cautious courtship ritual in detail.[53] For the purposes of the following reading, the central point of interest lies with what is there, in the entity of the film, 'things that I believe to be in the film for all to see, and to see the sense of'.[54] Whatever the wrangling or restraints, the artists and consultants have determined certain collections of colours, and presented a picture for our appraisal. I'm interested in the way *Written on the Wind* applies Technicolor's riches to create complex studies of demonstrative behaviour. Here, as a crucial element of mise-en-scène, dazzling colour expresses the impact of ostentation as well as more insidious schemes. In this film, brash displays are subtly revealing.

Beginnings and endings

As the opening musical theme chimes and booms its doom-laden refrain, the images form their own overture of the film's concerns. Like the horns and drums, Technicolor's bold tones feature prominently in each composition. The film begins as it ends, with signs of a man trapped by the recklessness of his life and death. Kyle Hadley is out of control, and yet bound to an inevitable fate. The opening sequence captures both aspects at once, of being careless and caught. In the mid-distance of dawn's gloom, a bright yellow roadster careers into the town of Hadley. The breakneck pace of the hurtling car introduces a film and character in constant forward motion: tearing into town, flying into restaurants, soaring into blue skies, landing in Miami and tripping across the world, only to blow with shrouds of dead leaves into the family seat, where all will stop. The colour of the car matches the yellow of the film's many taxicabs, materialising on command to whisk the characters towards and away from each other, to and from their fortunes.

In scorching yellow, Hadley brands the landscape. The fierce pace of the opening moments complements a quick compression of details. *Written on the Wind* situates its protagonist in lightning speed. Shot by shot, the film links the space and the driver ever more tightly. Kyle's blaze through the town-with-his-name allows for the disclosure of more features, as if in sweeping contemptuous declaration of ownership, of all that he surveys. First, the car dashes past one of many oil-pumps. As the heavy pump dips and rises in rhythmic labour, its mechanical nod appears a dutiful acknowledgement of the master's passing. The authority of Kyle in and over the landscape gains fuller expression in the sight of the signature circular red 'H' on the side of a nearby container. 'H' is for Hadley. The circle's stamp will appear in many shots from now on, as if the family of magnates owns the film itself. As the roadster whips along the road, under a skyline of oil scaffolds, it arcs by Hadley headquarters. A mile-high neon 'H' crests the monolithic structure, burning white-hot to blink on and off, fuelled by its powerful product. The journey ends with a close-up of Kyle, the first of the film. Swigging from a bottle of whisky, he spits the cork onto the road, his road. Alongside a heady impression of Hadley's authority, there is also an underlying sense of powerlessness. The shots of the roadster tracing and racing along the road cast different angles. Together, they tangle like the mesh of a spider's web. The idea develops in the film's positioning of a horizon of oil scaffolds, their intricate metalwork lacing across the skyline. Kyle is caught in a web of his own making. The sporty roadster becomes an instrument of another's sport, perhaps, as 'flies to wanton boys'.

To close the opening credits, through sounds, gestures, and colours, the sense of tension couples with that of release. As the roadster slips into the family driveway, a high wave of horns on the musical soundtrack suddenly breaks, dipping and softening. The fanfare gives way to the crooning voices of The Four Aces. The film cuts to its first view of family friend Mitch Wayne (Rock Hudson), standing in the window, waiting for Kyle's return. On the cut, The Four Aces sing 'A faithless lover's kiss is written on the wind', and an unspoken love story begins (and ends). The film moves quickly from Mitch's watchful gaze to a close-up of the roadster's front lights, glaring into the lens. With a slight tilt, the camera brings in the front windows of the house, brightly lit in a matching yellow flare. Here, *Written on the Wind* declares a particular interest in bright lights and shades of yellow. In its intrusiveness, the colour probes. Yet in its intensity, it blinds. The first sight of the two female protagonists – Kyle's wife, Lucy Moore (Lauren Bacall), and his sister, Marylee Hadley – deepens and complicates the handling of colour. Waiting for Kyle in her bed under worried sheets, Lucy wears a light yellow nightshirt and a long-suffering expression of anxiety. The deep red of the bed's headboard overpowers the yellow of the shirt. The scenario heralds many occasions in the film in which Lucy rests against a red backing, in beds, on chairs, in cars. Overwhelmed, Lucy collapses in a swoon, tumbling down on the bed. In turn, Kyle's own act of release gains hold of the whole house. Finishing the whisky, he hurls the empty bottle at the facing wall. As the bottle smashes down, two darkened basement windows suddenly glow in yellow light. The contemptuous act of Kyle 'killing' a bottle of whisky brings the house to life, and pre-empts his death. Finally, Marylee makes an appearance. Slyly creeping to her bedroom window, her eyes are covered by a band of sickly yellow light. Crafty and curious, she is blinded by contempt. All in the house are alert and inquisitive at just the point that Kyle's sense slips away.

Lose; see more

With dying leaves scattered in the vestibule, the wind blows the calendar back from November 1956 to October 1955. The pull backward through time heralds the proper introduction of Lucy Moore, as the executive secretary of a Hadley director. Her meticulousness carries and controls the moment. With a soft waft of her hand and the accompaniment of a musical flourish, she neatly traces a pen across her diary page. Much more lightly than the branding of a yellow sports car or red Hadley 'H', Lucy makes her mark on the film. Like the music, the camera appears enchanted by this woman, moving with her so very gently and easily, yet with poise, too. It tilts to follow her hand across the desk, coming to rest on a bold red placard, a mock-up advertising board for Hadley Oil. As if they were opening a waltz, camera and character rise and arc onto the floor in concert. Favouring finesse over fussiness, Lucy finds room to dance through her duties. She pivots left and right, holding the placard aloft, checking the details. In her writing, movement, and appraisal of the artwork, everything is effortlessly composed. After a light step across the room, a slight flick of the wrist clips the fluent movement. In a quietly revealing gesture, careful Lucy carelessly dumps the placard down on a chair: a little fall from grace.

Colour is crucial to the act's significance, and opens a key motif. The red of the placard is one of a small number of colours that connects Lucy and Kyle in particular ways. The shifts in Lucy's treatment of the placard (and colour) encapsulate her complicated future relationship with the brash millionaire. First, there is the cautious scrutiny of the bold sign, its bright attractions kept at arm's length. Then, there is the dumping down, hinting at a disregard for the showy mock-up. At the same time, this little dismissal contains a sense of release, as if habitual measures of control are relaxed under the sway of the sign. Kyle Hadley's colourful designs will cause Lucy to let go. The dropped placard sits under a row of similar boards, set on easels across the centre of the room: red, yellow, and orange [see plate 22]. Each carries a crude image: a car, a tanker, two jet planes. The simple images have a toy-like quality that recalls the sight of Kyle's speeding roadster. In turn, they deepen the notion of a childish playboy at the helm of a powerful machine. As if flushed by the hot colours of these gaudy designs, Lucy moves to slide the window open just a crack more. She arches her hand to smooth her hair, rearranging the placards, setting all in place again.

As she becomes lost in Kyle's rich and glossy world, Lucy will see more, and see less clearly. Mitch Wayne catches sight of her first. As this initial encounter plays out, a more implicit relationship develops in the background. At the moment of meeting, the film holds Lucy and Mitch in mid-shot, presenting both characters' bits of business at once. Rearranging the placards, Lucy doubles the number of red designs on display,

4.1 *Written on the Wind* (Douglas Sirk, 1956)

just as Mitch walks through the door. Although a minor gesture, the film builds on the gradual push of more reds in the frame, with the bold hue showily standing in for Kyle, between just these two characters. Lucy's position behind the billboards also means that Mitch cannot see her directly. In a move to close shot, a cubist painting acts as Mitch's backdrop. There are frames within frames here: of the film, of the painting, of a picture within the painting. The latter comprises slabs of yellow, red, blue, and green, the central colours of the film. Mitch and the camera sneak a peek at Lucy's legs under the border of the billboards. The oblique angles and flashes of colour mimic the cubist impulses of the painting. It is a playful gesture of seeing a familiar setting from a new angle. Lucy's appearance in the office is a beguiling surprise. Her relationship with Mitch starts from an odd position, and will become increasingly fractured when Kyle meets her too.

Red backdrops and cloths

The closer Lucy gets to Kyle the more the reds brood. A pattern of red picks up as she agrees to accompany Mitch to the restaurant '21', where Kyle waits for him.[55] Wryly commenting on Kyle's indulgences – travelling 1580 miles for a steak sandwich – they rest back on the deep red leather seating. The image recalls the shape and hue of earlier instances. When Mitch and Lucy meet in her office, the colourful placards stand between them. There is also a rhyme with the initial view of Lucy in the credit sequence, tumbling down on her red-backed bed. Like Kyle, red stresses the characters' arrangements by implication. The tone of a conversation can become tainted by thoughts of an illustrious figure, especially in their absence. In the taxi, Lucy smiles in accord with Mitch's remark that they might be 'two of a kind'. The bright redness of her lipstick plays off the richer, darker shade of the leather seating. Although they are not yet aware of it, they will become two of a kind only in their link to Kyle. The colour forms a backdrop to an overwrought relationship. Even

4.2 *Written on the Wind* (Douglas Sirk, 1956)

before these three people come together, Mitch and Lucy are
indirectly associated with Kyle's brashness.

The shifting tone of Lucy and Kyle's first encounter forms
in red flushes for both of them. There is the flush to mark a
sudden intense feeling, the beginning of an exciting period, a
sudden increased number of things, and the flush that causes
one to become red in the face. Initially, red only fringes the
frame and scene, on a low, slow burn. In the restaurant, Kyle
sits with two female companions. The brightness of the occasion is on the verge of petering out. All three stare into their
drinks, down to the flat surface and red edge of the tablecloth.
As if by magic, the appearance of Mitch and Lucy instantly
picks them up and fans the flames. Kyle conjures Mitch up
in a dreamy account ('the kind of assets he's got you can't buy
for money'). As thoughts turn to this 'sidekick', the camera
drifts left with a waft of cigarette smoke to reveal the couple,
just as they appear. On seeing them, a tipsy Kyle lifts his head
and rises up, dipping his cigarette down to fizzle in a glass
of champagne. The moment is as loaded as the host, full of
drink, dreams, power, and impotence.

A new vibrancy comes with a change in perspective and an
upsurge of red tones. The previous, dull party is put out with
the dunked butt, making way for more audacious designs.
Kyle greets and leads his new guests to a clean table. Wealth's

enchantment touches the scene. The film does not make the change of tables clear. There is the suggestion that the two tedious girls have simply disappeared. The sparkle of fresh champagne takes their place, magically appearing in the melt of a dissolve. Before the new glasses materialise, as the new threesome sits, the camera tilts to loom over the tablecloth. Whereas the red cloth previously added only an edge of colour, it now fills the frame in a burst of brightness [see plate 23]. Here is the first flush – too much. As the camera tips into the dazzling red surface, it threatens to overwhelm. The move matches the effect of Kyle's own grandiose gestures; both over-reach.

For Lucy, the day's dealings are undeniably exciting, yet Kyle's showy boasts and shallow clichés are embarrassing. Held for a beat too long, the commanding shot of the red cloth is suggestively emphatic. The dissolve brings the champagne glasses into view over the dense red block. Together, the moves are declamatory and mysterious. As the camera tips, colour swells and glasses gradually appear. Meaning is at once suspended, opaque, and dissolved. While Kyle remains steadfast in his self-belief, the looming camera fleetingly and forcefully marks a little crisis. It urges attention and yet the significance of these urges remains unspecified. As in many other films, the future of two lovers hinges on the form of their first meeting. Here, a first encounter balances precariously – as Lucy and Kyle's relationship will do – between crude declarations and more tacit disturbances.

Up in the blue

Technicolor's bold palette complicates instances when Kyle asserts his 'true colours'. A good example comes with a concerted effort by the character to lift the mood and advance his designs on Lucy. The exchange begins with Kyle's proclamation to Lucy, by way of persuading her to fly with him to Miami, that 'once we get up in the blue I'm a different fella'. The firm belief in showing entirely separate colours, shuttling between self-contained personalities, fits with the magnate's crude outlook on life. (As Mitch disparagingly notes of Kyle's behaviour, 'simple ... or should I say simplistic'). It points towards a state of self-delusion. Kyle's airborne trip 'up in the blue' begins a flight of fantasy that involves all three protagonists. Lucy's whirlwind journey to riches and despair is first set in motion as she steps back into another taxi, this time with Kyle. Lucy's tentative acceptance of the invitation is enough for Kyle; in a dissolve, the couple appear by the plane. Kyle's eager determination clips away time.

The film first appears to encourage Kyle's delusion, quickly switching the colours that accompany him on the private jet from reds to blues. Gleefully ushering Lucy onto the plane, Kyle opens the passenger door. As the tin portico arches across on the hinge, the signature red Hadley 'H' on its hard exterior surface is instantly replaced with the padded blue fabric of its inner side [see plates 24 and 25]. Kyle's demeanour swings with the door, just like that. Following Kyle's little admission that he drinks too much, Lucy succumbs. Stooping to enter the aircraft, their matching light grey jackets brush together. Mitch's surprise presence quickly complicates the moment of parity. His jacket, tawny-brown, fits with the interior of the plane. He is, perhaps reluctantly, somewhat at home in this familiar place. Whilst accustomed to these confines, he muddies the new light tone of the fledgling relationship, standing in between Lucy and Kyle in the overcrowded cabin. A block of blue, Kyle's (new) blue returns as he reclaims authority of the occasion. Directing Lucy into the cockpit, he shuts the door on his other passenger. Through the cabin's window, Kyle and Lucy are placed before a wash of blue light. Blue horizons pattern across the film, framed in windows, doorways and on verandas, always just out of reach for one or all of the characters, hazily tantalising with impossible desires.

As the film moves into the cockpit, other colours spill into Kyle's fabrication of the 'different fella'. Tones filtering on the couple's faces change with those of the conversation.

Lucy starts to let her guard down. She responds favourably to Kyle's clichéd line ('you know, I've seen you before ... in the office'). Her pale skin and silvery blouse complement the pastel peach and blue horizon in the window. Up in the air, Lucy's determination softens. She allows herself a little light flirtation. Yet, hints of yellow light up Kyle's face, traces of our earlier sighting of his later self perhaps, of the runaway roadster and wild-eyed glares. He could flare up.

The arrangement of colours taints Kyle's 'simple tale' of friendship and family. Now the film reframes to place him against the blue skies. The scene is set for misty-eyed reminiscence. We learn that Kyle and Mitch were childhood pals, that Kyle wished Mitch's dad was his own, that only Mitch measures up to his father's hopes. Mitch, Mitch, Mitch. Kyle is absorbed in his melancholy tale. Lucy shares the glow from the window, enlightened and dazzled at the same time. A final shift blocks out the blue mood and closes thoughts of Mitch (just as the film cuts to him in cargo, snapping shut a heavy book). To raise spirits and with a glint in his eye, Kyle turns from confession back to clichés. Ablaze once more with the boastfulness of '21', Kyle self-consciously spins yarns of derring-do. Suddenly, an intense red light burns on his face, beaming with his grin. The film's abrupt and blatant display of rich red colour calls attention to the forced manner of Kyle's affectations. It matches his broad stories of gambling, red for the roulette squares. Kyle warms to thoughts of chancing his luck with Lucy. The colour sears through his overplayed descriptions of fiendish behaviour: 'Hellfire, they'd be disappointed if I didn't behave like a playboy, didn't end up like my uncle ... My kid sister Marylee, she's got enough devil in her to put Uncle Joe and me in the shade. What's the matter, your ears burning?' Kyle is not being devilish here – he just thinks he is, lost in his own imagery. He spoils the portrait of the 'different fella' in a moment of colourful indulgence.

Mitch's entry into the cockpit closes the scene and adds a final complex of colour. The tale of three black sheep in the Hadley family gives way to a trio caught in their own tainted romance. Mitch leans through the cockpit hatch, breaking in on the various reveries with news that they are approaching Miami. As the announcement unsettles Lucy, the film reveals an even more awkward position, encapsulating the threesome's situation. Whereas Kyle turns with ease to see and speak with Mitch (in a ribbing aside), Lucy must crane back, away from the horizon. The framing of several shots sets the three in a triangle, each steeped in a different colour [see plate 26]. Lucy has her head in the clouds, blue from Kyle's sad boasts. Kyle still smarts red. Mitch is in yellow, witnessing once again the sickly display of Hadley's charm offensive.

Floods of colour

Both film and Kyle ready themselves for a showcase moment, displaying their riches. As the canvas broadens in the trip to Miami, the colour scheme becomes more prolific. Whilst the range is extensive, each colour is also concentrated, matching the intensification of Kyle's lusty plans. Sprays of colour shower the frame, designed to overpower and woo. The visual impact of these bright cascades is instantaneous, yet their emergence is not; everything is pre-arranged. The first hints of Kyle's crafty preparations arrive with the travellers in the airport lounge. Lucy and Mitch sit amongst the crowds. Everyone is dressed in drab patterns of brown and grey. The film frames Kyle in the background, in a telephone booth, calling ahead to the hotel. The link of Kyle, red and backdrops comes to the fore again. As he giddily makes his ostentatious arrangements over the phone, flashes of red appear amongst the duller colours: on a pilot's cap, a neck-scarf, a passer-by's dress. His excitement cannot help but boil over into the scene, stimulating the tired surroundings. Lucy's lipstick tones in too, as one of the few red frissons. She is warming to Kyle's ways, a touch thrilled by this big adventure.

A quiver of pleasure turns to a shock of colours in the hotel suite. It is a scene of enticement and exposure, of Kyle overwhelming Lucy with displays of largesse. The movements of camera and characters chart a series of urges, building as they draw deeper into the room. Each push forward reveals more flushes of colour. The scene starts off-key. The 'Hadley red' now turns a sickly puce, washed across the hotel lobby's walls. The note of disturbance lingers on in the paler pink walls of the suite. Music and mood start low, also in a minor key. Lucy is unmoved. Yet, the room and moment are arranged to beguile, to open up like a music box. As the crafts-man of these rich enchantments, an undeterred Kyle steps in to set things off, turning on the bedroom light. As if cued by the move, the musical soundtrack brightens to add its own twinkle: the music box springs to life. Kyle's gesture sparks Lucy's attention. The camera edges with her into the suite, its move bringing in a border of red flowers and the pert gold stem of a champagne bottle. The colours are compelling; the more Lucy is drawn in, the more they saturate. As if taking a breath before the plunge, she wavers then drifts with the camera through the room. A heady mix of pinks, purples, oranges, and reds floods the frame [see plate 27]. Flowers and fruits tumble together in elaborate arrangements, and the music swirls in eddies. After a little encouragement, Lucy's momentum carries her. Although her face reveals a note of reticence, she doesn't resist the tug; Kyle sweeps her into the bedroom, opening up more and more compartments of golden trinkets. Pushing ever further into the garish fantasy, Lucy is twice turned away from the ocean. The waters glow blue through the suite's windows, against the wealth of bright diversions inside. For Lucy, to embrace this opulent lifestyle is to risk turning her back on remote hopes of hidden depths.

At the end of the scene, Lucy stands alone on the balcony, on the verge of a decision. Touched with traces of the low blue light, she realises that the 'different fella' seen up in the skies is a faint promise, an unattainable idea that she holds dear. She flees the suite. Only when Kyle chases after her to the airport do the blue tones return to hold sway. Once again,

Lucy's better judgement clouds over. With remorseful words and on the cusp of romance, the film places the couple in front of a vast blue pane, looking out onto the airstrip. The fable of a happy future ('not to play, but to work, to behave') absorbs the couple.

Under the pink

Embracing the Technicolor spectrum, *Written on the Wind* introduces pinks in sparing amounts and indirect ways. This decision allows for hints of the colour's significance to build before more abundant applications assert their hold. Pinks gradually collect around the character of Marylee Hadley, Kyle's 'kid sister'. There is a glimpse of Marylee in the opening credits, her wild eyes fixed in gleaming light. Kyle refers to her fleetingly in the private jet, as one of the unholy trinity of Hadley devils. Both allusions are brief, yet linger in the mind. Increasingly, whispers of pink pry into arrangements, just as Marylee interferes in the affairs of others. The influence of colour and character grows by insinuation. Then their presence becomes persistent. After all, Marylee takes over.

Properties of pink complement Marylee's personality. Both appear delicate but sheer. Both are frivolous, constantly flirting for attention. In any given scenario, their effervescence cajoles, or more irritatingly needles. Aspects twist together. Pink can be the colour of carefree play, of kids-stuff, candy-stripes and sweet talk. It is also giddy and heady, the fizz of pink champagne or the racy spoils of a Cadillac. As a flesh tone, the connotations can be lustier, too. In this film, tints of pink taint lives.

Marylee's spiteful intrusions are not the sole cause of the characters' downfall, but like the accompanying pink frills, they ruffle on the way to ruin. The entry of colour and character in the 'second act' of the film is appropriately sly. Kyle and Lucy are now married, jetting off on honeymoon. The scene opens on Mitch packing up in his Miami hotel room, uprooted by the news of his friend's wedding ('right under my nose'). In a long shot and looking for answers, a snooping reporter pokes his head round the door. Sneaking into the private quarters, his move reveals a chink of pink from the adjacent hotel lobby walls. The colour is furtively associated with acts of stealth and exposure. The film quickly couples the suggestion with a cheeky peek at the newlyweds lying in their marital bed. All seems restful. The fairytale hopes of the honeymoon gather in blue horizons: a Kubla Khan vista of cerulean palms and azure waters. Pinks infuse the scene, too, in the glow of the lovers' bare skin against white linen. Although light, the colour is pressing. As Lucy brushes across Kyle to raise his sleepy head, she discovers a pistol under his pillow. Again, a touch of pink leads to an unsettling revelation.

Having tinged pinks with signs of trouble, the film edges Marylee into the picture. Like the previous sightings of pink, her arrival marks an indirect disturbance. Mitch receives a call from bartender Dan (Robert J. Wilke). Marylee is making a nuisance of herself, drunkenly flirting with a local no-good, Roy Carter (John Larch). Even her name comes at one remove, in an allusion to 'the Hadley gal'. As Dan sends the news, the camera steals left to show Marylee coiled in a snug, framed in the bar-room mirror. Far left of the shot, her image reflects back as a dab of pink and a sheaf of blonde hair [see plate 28]. Like a blip on the radar, the brief glimpse punctuates lengthier, weightier scenes of Kyle introducing Lucy to his father, and Mitch's grand plans for the oil company. Springing up out of nowhere, it is a bothersome interruption of the day's bigger business, but it cuts to the quick. Marylee's blithe cruelty gashes into the film. Professing boredom to her oily companion, she carelessly slashes a knife across the snug table. A misspent afternoon with Roy Carter is just one more notch on her bedpost, designed to get on Kyle's nerves. Marylee likes spoiling things, always looking to score quick points off her brother, or slyly win Mitch's notice. Her vicious little outbursts leave ugly marks. As Kyle and Mitch hurry to the bar, *finally* Marylee gets a little attention. Fists fly, knives and guns are pulled, but Marylee wears the scene lightly. She drapes across the frames of men and furnishings in her pink chiffon scarf: loose around the edges, yet with a chokehold.

It is as if the film starts again, just for her. The fight was a sugary rush, pink and giddy, turning queasy. Never mind; it did the trick, Mitch is here. Instantly forgotten, the scene is replaced by another brash confection. With a blast of brass on the soundtrack and a saccharine grin, Marylee glows with brazen delight, perched in her off-pink sports car. Three shades of pink collide in the driving seat. As if concussed by the heady mix, Mitch is swayed over. Bounding up, he shows a glimmer of boyish affection for this flighty girl. As he clambers into the car, a pair of red socks peek out underneath more understated khaki work-pants. It is a sign of a previous, more naïve kinship with the Hadleys. Right on cue, Marylee chirps out an old refrain:

> Mitch, let's go down to the river, to our old haunt. We used to be happy there. Our own private world, mine and yours, and Kyle's. Then you grew up and left me ... I guess that's why I hate him so. For taking you away from me ... I'll have you, marriage or no marriage.

Having lingered in the background for so long, Marylee now audaciously reveals her intentions. The camera cuts to close shot; the brash tones suddenly magnify. For the first time in the film, a shock of pinks seizes the moment, making the boldest statement.

An insidious sense of determination follows, forming in blushes rather than bluster. Her mind now set, Marylee schemes to manipulate by insinuation. Rumours of pink infuse her rising appearances. Immediately following her boastful announcement, Marylee materialises in Lucy's dressing room. It seems 'the Hadley gal' has the same darkly magical gift as her brother, eliding time to promote her plans. A wand waves somewhere off-screen, adding a touch of charm and trickery. Marylee's presence carries in the texture of pink materials. The colour dyes the cotton towel carried by Lucy, an easy chair, and the net drapes on the windows. It covers and wraps as lightly as Marylee inveigles. The film amuses itself with the female characters' parallel appearances: their white blouses are very much alike; a mirror image of Marylee tousles her hair just as Lucy does the same. The spell cannot sustain this self-consciousness. With Marylee's increasingly rude chatter, rather than flatter, the gathering blushes of pink start to impose. In a final blast of impertinence, Marylee flounces out under a swathe of pink silk. Her visit has become nothing more than a lightly veiled threat.

In a public setting, blushes complicate the formal composure of the Hadleys' 'Anniversary Ball'. Pinks are immediately apparent and discreetly unsettling. As the scene opens, a candy-pink cabriolet delivers more guests before slipping away. Having made itself known, the colour withdraws from centre stage. Similarly, rather than drive this event, Marylee first circles and lurks. The camera also takes an unobtrusive approach. Instead of sweeping into the ball through the grand front entrance, it sidles through a window. The significance of the ball opens up obliquely. A little verbal pun leads the way. As the camera dips through the window, it seizes on a clutch of giddy guests, chattering about a football game. Holding out her hands in pantomime exasperation, rising into her partner's arms, a rather limp guest declares, 'I never know who's got the ball'. In the centre of the gathering, blonde on black, stands Marylee. The delivery of the line heralds more rising guests and musical notes, taking up the refrain to circle around the Hadley gal, pushing in on her. Refusing to allow her brother's celebration to encroach on her own plans, Marylee, like the pink cab, steals away from the hordes. Game on.

A retreat allows for a regrouping: pinks tinge a more private space before spilling back into the open arena. Marylee creeps into the shadows of Mitch's old bedroom, teasing light into the gloomy cloisters. A wash of blue soaks the nostalgic scenario, the space of 'so many wonderful afternoons' – another lost dream. Pink sprinklings dust the scene as Marylee skirts the room: rose peeks of a sofa arm, glimpses of shoulders, neck, the rounds of her breasts. As if ready for her close-up, she moves in for the kill. All of a sudden, a beaming Marylee sidles up to Mitch. Splendidly lit, her diamonds twinkle and her black dress bleeds into the shaded décor, leaving only the flush of her body. It is a moment of overexposure. Flirtation gives way to amplification. Marylee openly propositions Mitch before deriding her 'idiot brother' and his naïve wife. Rejected, she bursts back into the ball and onto the dance-floor. She reworks and exaggerates her dance in front of Mitch as a supercharged rumba. Her earlier moves failed; now is the time to improvise, to take prime position. There is an unhinged flare to Marylee's furious display. As she moves, twists of pink and red fabric tumble in the frame. A bop of hot-pinks leads into Kyle's red-faced discovery that a 'condition' prevents him from having children. Like a malevolent rain-dance, his sister's performance summons a psychological storm.

Another frenzied display of Marylee's dancing marks a final twist in the plot. Kyle's inability to cope with the news of his condition leads him back to drink, and to feverish boyhood dreams of Mitch. Marylee continues to infuriate the family, picking up a young petrol attendant in her little pink car before heading home in disgrace, escorted by the Hadley police. In the deceptive quiet of the aftermath, Marylee performs a death-dealing jive. The act brings about her father's demise, a literal downfall, plummeting to his death down the Hadley mansion's high stairway. The delirious scene seems to spring out of nowhere, striking like a viper, recoiling as quickly too. It plays out as an acid temper tantrum, spiked with the jagged beats of the music and Marylee's venomous contempt. It has a hallucinatory quality, at once impressionistic and intensely concentrated. Whilst the film sustains previous patterns of colour and meaning, it allows the moment to slip away from the realm of the representational. In this instant, just as the order of things breaks down, *Written on the Wind* moves into abstraction.

4.3 *Written on the Wind* (Douglas Sirk, 1956)

There are warning signs in colours from the outset.
Washes of blue previously appear in moments of quiet intro-
spection and wistful reminiscence. There is a similar tinge to
Marylee's room, yet the scene's tone is very different. Rather
than mooning after times past, Marylee now dances on the
grave of memories: to hell with the lot of them. Moving
swiftly away from the blue, the camera reveals an unusually
pallid setting. Sheer white walls and a bone-white gown present blank surfaces on which Marylee can scrawl her spite.
She dips to light her cigarette in white-hot flames. A shimmy
across the floor and on goes the record player. As the camera
tilts and horns flare up, fierce red lily heads appear as violent
blotches against the white background. There is something
odd about these rubbery flowers, as if drawn by a sulky child:
hastily sketched, crudely coloured, and oversized. A strange
white bust, an approximation of a human head, accompanies
the lilies on the dresser. It is an incoherent tableau, as wrong-
headed as the dance. The dance is a striptease that stops her
father's heart. Using her display case as a screen, Marylee
wraps herself in a flimsy peach nightgown, swirling and
turning. The sensation of the moment envelops her. The flick
of the earlier pink flounce in Lucy's bedroom now becomes a
riotous fandango. As the music builds and her father climbs
the stairs to silence her, Marylee rocks and twitches like an

animal in death-throes. The camera cuts closer, dangerously close to the whirl of pink limbs under the billowing peach gown. The film moves to an extreme position of heightened colour and emotion. It borders on hysteria, with form and feelings becoming both intense and confused. As the moment threatens to tear the fabric of the film's world, the father topples to his death. Marylee collapses onto a chair, kicking her legs up in a gleeful pink fit [see plate 29].

A concentration on colour opens up the film's complexities to the last, even in demonstratively climactic moments. Events unfold to turn the film back to the opening images. Kyle wrongly assumes that Mitch is the father of Lucy's unborn child, and seeks revenge. The yellow roadster turns once more into the Hadley driveway, waking the house. In a fumbling tussle, Kyle shoots himself dead. With father and older sibling gone, all power shifts to Marylee. The final image of her is both bombastic and intricate in its treatment of colour. In medium shot and a stiffly pinched grey suit, Marylee sits gravely at her father's desk. In dress, posture and gesture she apes her father's portrait hanging on the wall behind. Both are hunched, clasping a miniature mock-up of an oil scaffold [see plate 30]. The rhyme is blatant, and blatantly asserted – a fittingly ugly end – but there is more. Marylee grips and strokes the erect scaffold with one firm push to the shaft. The film is unabashed in its phallic symbolism. Yet, further, diffuse suggestions lie in the colour of the object, too. The miniature scaffold is a bright yellow plaything for Marylee, held tightly in her hand. Just as the film's ending inevitably meets the beginning, the prominent appearance of the replica scaffold recalls the first image: a pint-sized yellow roadster swerving across the industrial landscape. Whereas Kyle's boys-toy belittles the man, racing him to his end, Marylee becomes the player, not the played. Tucked behind lustier suggestions, a book-ending rhyme of colours and trappings reveals Marylee as rueful puppeteer, seeking relief in her spoils.

5 *Fear Eats the Soul*
(Rainer Werner Fassbinder:
Germany, 1974)

'I hope or think that I conform as little as possible.'
(Rainer Werner Fassbinder)[56]

'Don't mention foreign workers. It makes him see red.'
(Krista (Irm Hermann), *Fear Eats the Soul*)

In his entry on Rainer Werner Fassbinder in *The New Biographical Dictionary of Film,* David Thomson writes:

> There can be no doubt about the opportunities German cinema offered in the 1970s to politically committed but formally experimental films ... [Fassbinder] was an exponent of pure film, minus vibrato or expressiveness, so uncompromisingly plain that we rediscover social realism beneath all the petty guises of life's performance ... His style was antistyle.[57]

The following reading of *Fear Eats the Soul* sees colour as crucial to the apparently contradictory elements of Fassbinder's powerful 'antistyle'. Fassbinder's aesthetic is rife with impulses pushing in different directions: putative opposites that somehow mesh. Thomson describes a cinema of social realism and formal experimentalism. Fassbinder fills everyday settings with artifice and illusion to get to life's truths. His films comprise an immersion in the plastic arts of cinema, celebrating the medium's potentialities even as they pull it apart. Thomson adds an evocative description of these contrary drives in relation to another of Fassbinder's

films, *The Bitter Tears of Petra von Kant* (1972), noting that
'[it] still has no equal in its simultaneous delight in "style"
while pouring acid over the image.'[58] There are also apparent contradictions in style and meaning. This is a cinema of
exhibitionism exploring aspects of privacy, a site of alienation
housing portraits of human intimacy.

Fassbinder after Sirk

A consideration of *Fear Eats the Soul* after *Written on the Wind*
matches Fassbinder's ardent following of Douglas Sirk's
melodramatic art. Fassbinder's love of Sirk's work is well
known.[59] Rather than adhering to the principles of realist or
Marxist filmmaking to present his biting accounts of German
society, Fassbinder adopts the seemingly contrary position of
overt melodramatic stylisation. He recasts Sirk's aesthetic via
German culture, pushing against the thrust of more overt
intellectual cinema prevalent in the 1960s. In Fassbinder's
films, radicalism comes through his reshaping of the popu-
lar, populist form of classical Hollywood melodrama.

As we have seen, *Written on the Wind* (as a melodrama
of the 1950s) offers exemplary renderings of 'emotional and
psychological predicaments' externalised in décor, gesture,
and colour. Taking advantage of similar designs, Fassbinder's
films use Sirk's visual language to convey arrested or inter-
nalised feelings of love, loneliness, hatred, and prejudice. In
the cinematic worlds presented by both Sirk and Fassbinder,
just as the characters are suffocating in their domestic
lives and homes, their stifled emotions structure the mise-
en-scène. However, in Fassbinder's films, the expressive
relationship of décor and colour to character becomes problematic. The stylistic conventions of melodrama combine
with Brechtian processes of distanciation.[60] Simultaneously,
the style draws us closer to the characters' inner feelings and
holds us apart.

Thomson captures part of this stylistic confrontation in his
Dictionary entry: 'Time and again, Fassbinder's characters

1 The Green Ray

2–5 Three Colours: White

6

7

8

9

6–9 *Equinox Flower*

10

11

12

10–12 *Equinox Flower*

13 *The Green Ray*

14

15

16 **17**

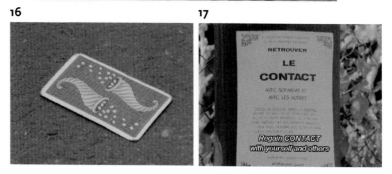

14–17 *The Green Ray*

18

19

20   **21**

18–21 *The Green Ray*

22–30 *Written on the Wind*

28

29

30

31

32

31–32 *Fear Eats the Soul*

33

34

35

36

33–36 *The Umbrellas of Cherbourg*

sit around a table, apparently exchanging commonplaces. They are filmed as flatly as possible, denied facial expressiveness, and ordered to stylize flaccid dialogue with crazy rhythm. This is both an alienation effect and a dramatization of Fassbinder's view of our demoralized lives.'[61] A robotic handling of performative elements exploits their particular expressive possibilities. While melodramatic style is evoked and dispelled, the barriers of extreme stylisation reveal the characters' difficult experience of being honest – with themselves, with each other – in a confrontational world. Freedom of expression, say Fassbinder's films, is hard to achieve in a society that values, above all else, displays of conformity. Their style corresponds to this interrogation of compliance. Colour is the key to a better understanding of these stylistic, psychological, and social blockades.

A short tough tale

This reading of *Fear Eats the Soul* is presented as a short, dense take on one of Fassbinder's 'short, tough tales.'[62] It concentrates on one scene that takes place in a café courtyard. The chapter is also presented in light of one previous example of critical writing on the same sequence. The piece is by Julian Savage and appears in the sleeve-notes to the Arrow Films DVD of *Fear Eats the Soul* (see Appendix A). Savage notes how:

> In a scene from Fassbinder's *Fear Eats the Soul*, Emmy, an aging, widowed German national, and Ali, a much younger Moroccan immigrant, sit together at an outdoor café. They are encircled by an arrangement of yellow chairs; stark horizontal and vertical slats seem to entrap them. The waiters refuse to serve. Fortified in this fortress of yellow (the colour of fear, perhaps), drooping trees weigh down upon them as they are almost consumed by their surroundings.[63]

As described, *Fear Eats the Soul* tells a story of ageism and racial prejudice, focusing on the difficult relationship of an elderly cleaning lady and a young Moroccan man. The film's

Sirkian interest in visually evoking states of repression, social
and emotional, comes to the fore in Savage's reading. For
Savage, the lovers' surroundings ensnare and engulf them. A
more sustained appraisal of the moment, its colouring, and
its impact presents further complexities.

The scene marks a pivotal point in the narrative. Having
married Ali (El Hedi ben Salem) and, consequently, met the
racist reaction of her family, neighbours, and workmates,
Emmi (Brigitte Mira) breaks down. In the large courtyard,
she declares her love for Ali, her hatred of the 'swine' waiters
watching on in disgust, and suggests a holiday: 'let's go away
somewhere. Somewhere where we'll be on our own, where
no one knows us, and no-one stares. When we get back it'll
all be different. Everyone will be nice to us. They will.' And
they are. The film drains the colours in the moment's fading
seconds and, for a beat, freezes the action: a chapter ends,
the holiday elided in the fade. As Emmi promises, everything changes afterwards, but not for the better. Her family
and friends find ways to insinuate themselves back into the
couple's lives, using them for various chores and duties.
Emmi and Ali exploit each other's affections.

The first image of the sequence self-consciously presents
a dramatic core. In long shot, the lovers sit holding hands
across one of many yellow tables [see plate 31]. Amidst all the
clutter, they are now at the centre of their relationship. Savage
suggests that Emmi and Ali are 'encircled by an arrangement
of yellow chairs; stark horizontal and vertical slats seem to
entrap them.' Such an understanding is led by the next shot
of the sequence. Over Ali's shoulder, the restaurant workers
watch the couple with fixed stares and stances. A subsequent
shot draws nearer to the workers, presenting a tableau of
mute contempt. Earlier in the film, there have been equally
uncomfortable instances in which the couple sit alone for
judgment (by us, by other characters), most notably when
they visit a restaurant apparently frequented in the past by
Hitler. Initially however, the courtyard scene paints a picture
of private intimacy. We soon learn that the camera adopts

5.1 *Fear Eats the Soul* (Rainer Werner Fassbinder, 1974)

the distant position of the contemptuous waiters, and we
witness Emmi's outpouring of distress. At first sight though,
the image is suggestive of a more compassionate scenario.
It appears that the couple have found, or been given, some
space of their own. It can even be read as a heightened romantic expression: all the other empty tables and chairs suggest
that, for these two people, the rest of the world has simply
disappeared. In the order of the shots – the couple holding
hands alone in the courtyard, *then* the hostile stares of the
waiters – the film proposes one extreme view only to replace
and efface it with its opposite. The world melts away for two
lovers; the world forces itself on them, with acute prejudice.

Feeling and noticing

The binding agent of these two starkly contrasting states,
the catalyst to complexity, is the colour. Fifty or so identically
coloured chairs and tables fill the frame, cast at bric-a-brac
angles. They all have white legs, but their yellow covers draw
the eye. A swathe of yellow confronts us. The impact is imme-
diate. (There are no shots leading up or into this space – it is

forcefully established in one image. Although unchanging, the view will inspire a range of different perspectives.) Associations of sickliness and peril may motivate Savage's reading of the colour as expressing uneasiness and entrapment (he proposes yellow as the colour of fear). The effect of the colour relies on the film's collisions of credibility and artifice. In writing about an example of 1950s Hollywood melodrama – *Bigger than Life* (Nicholas Ray, 1956) – V. F. Perkins notes a comparable occurrence:

> This [film] has a depressed middle-class setting. Its hero, a teacher with a heart ailment working to support his wife and young son, leaves school at the end of the day to start his evening job in the offices of a taxi company. As he walks away from the school building with its background of respectable greys and browns, the image dissolves into a general view of the cab-park photographed so that the screen is virtually covered with the garish yellow of the taxi-ranks. The transition thus handled gains an emotional colouring which conveys not only the physical strain under which the man lives, but also his *déclassé* feeling of shame in his secondary occupation. The colour here is 'natural'. It comes from an apparently objective recording of phenomena which we would expect to find in the settings presented: grey walls and dark brown doors on a school, bright yellow cabs in an (American) taxi pool. But it is just because we are not given reason to question the credibility of the colour that we can give the full emotional response that the arrangement of colour requires.[64]

Perkins then gives a contrasting example, of colour arrangements that 'by rejecting credibility, encourage a purely cerebral recognition':

> In Antonioni's *The Red Desert*, red is used to represent the threat which the neurotic heroine fears from an alienated, hostile and disintegrating world. Towards the end of the film she is made love to while on the verge of complete mental collapse. And from shot to shot the bedpost becomes an ever more threateningly glaring red. We observe that colour is being used to create an effect. Intellectually we can identify the effect required. But of the effect itself we feel no symptom. We are so busy *noticing*

that we respond rather to our awareness of the device than to the state of the mind it sets out to evoke.[65]

As part of Fassbinder's 'antistyle', the colours of *Fear Eats the Soul* (and of the café scene in particular) combine and complicate both types of aesthetic appeal. Like *Bigger than Life*, the sequence evokes 'physical strain' in the 'garish yellow' of the tables and chairs occupying the screen. Yet here, the 'emotional colouring' vacillates between subjects. There is the 'shame' projected on the lovers by the observing waiters. Then, there are also the pressures felt by the hurt couple, especially Emmi, physically and psychologically breaking down.

Similar to Perkins' example, the colour in the sequence comes from 'an apparently objective recording of phenomena which we would expect to find in the settings presented.' However, there are differences and difficulties. It is a given that many American taxicabs are yellow. Café furniture is sometimes painted yellow, but this is not always necessarily so (it could of course be any colour). The choice here is bright yellow, and it would be natural to see such a sunny colour used in a café courtyard. In its amount and exposure, as the screen is 'virtually covered' in yellow, the colour appears credible and peculiar. Rather than the usual colouring of an aesthetic object leading to dramatic meaning, the desertion of the tables and chairs makes their yellowness plain and arresting. While starkly presented as an 'apparently objective recording of phenomena', the courtyard seems in some way a distortion of reality. The tables' emptiness emphasises the colour's nakedness, makes it seem *too* stark and, in turn, the locale somehow strange. The décor is simultaneously within a normal state of affairs, as 'we would expect to find in the setting presented' and an unnatural contrivance. The wavering between states and understandings, of credibility and artifice, creates a layer of anxiety.

The obtrusive measures of yellow also court an intellectual response. Like the red bedpost example from Perkins' interpretation of a moment in *The Red Desert*, we can take the colour to represent alienation and hostility. Perkins' example is more akin to a 'special effect', but both appear in a similarly declamatory manner and give rise to thoughts about unnaturalness. The red bedpost, the yellow table sets, and, indeed, the contemptuous waiting staff are all 'threateningly glaring'. The naked yellow colouring expresses Emmi's vulnerable position 'on the verge of complete mental collapse.' In turn, 'intellectually we can identify the effect required.' If we follow Perkins further, we are thus so 'busy noticing' the yellow that 'we respond rather to our awareness of the device than to the state of mind it sets out to evoke.'

Here we are at the heart of Fassbinder's use of colour. Repeatedly across his films, tables, coverings, and the walls of empty or sparingly occupied settings appear in searing colours. These coloured surfaces are part of the normal state of things and look, in their sheerness, awkwardly or blatantly contrived. As a central element of the director's artistry, colour promotes a conflicting and sometimes violent set of responses. In treatment, it appeals to, is suspended somewhere between, heart and mind. In this moment from *Fear Eats the Soul*, we give the 'full emotional response that the arrangement of colour requires' while in 'awareness of the device'. We are caught up in (caught in the middle of) feeling and noticing.

In turn, the oscillation echoes the scene's contradictory reactions to love and hate, age and ageism, and, above all, race and racism. Emmi's exhausted declaration of love, self-doubt, and a frantic determination to flee causes jumbled feelings and words to spray out, mixing with the waiters' unspoken scorn. Watch Emmi's eyes when she rails against the 'swine'; she looks directly at Ali. Hysterical and in desperation, she then searches for 'practical' solutions: going on holiday, escaping familiar faces. The display is a frenzied confusion of passion and reason. The yellow colour clots together emotions and a complex of thought processes. Simultaneously, its conflicting effect – of feeling and noticing – confronts us with the experience of prejudice. By placing Emmi and Ali demonstratively in the centre, the film directs attention towards them. Then it emphasises this focus by showing the waiters' hostile looks. At the same time, the film stimulates an awkward reaction to colour, provoking the collision of emotional and cerebral responses. In so doing, it captures the contradictions of prejudice: the powerful tensions of passion and rationalisation engendered by intolerance.

If we connect the moment to later instances in the film, after the holiday, we also see a specific, discriminating affiliation of yellow around Emmi. Having soaked in a variance of extreme emotions and thoughts, in this later period, yellow meets a more insidiously diffuse attitude to the couple. The behavioural colouring of family and co-workers alters on their return. While reflecting on wider socio-political structures and values, thoughts in an interview between Peter W. Jansen and Fassbinder help make sense of the communal changes in *Fear Eats the Soul* following the courtyard scene:

> Jansen: Is there a reduction of freedom – you don't feel as free in Germany now?
> Fassbinder: Yes, I would say that. There is a definite reduction of freedom. *Some people really feel and notice it.* And the extent to which the others adapt their statements, be it concrete or their artistic statements, so as not to stand out, is another thing. The current climate leads to a kind of levelling, to the levelling of people ... this would lead to everybody looking, wearing, thinking the same.[66]

The earlier yellow reappears in more diminutive and everyday forms, most crucially on Emmi's clothing [see plate 32]. Rather than assailing the social, psychological, and cinematic status quo in confrontational blasts, yellow now colours less obtrusively, in a more restrained manner. Emmi's colouring suggests that, in adapting to the politely spiteful accommodations of her neighbours, the character enters into a tacit contract of compromise. They all internalise their ranging emotions, and a little of the noxious mix leaks out in their calculatedly reasonable behaviour. Adapting their statements, the characters kill each other with 'kindness.'

In the courtyard scene, an uncompromising display of yellow colour draws out conflicting impulses. It later reappears in a less arresting form to hint at the acidic hazards of concession. Because of the unrelenting amalgam of pressures presented in the café's court, love becomes intellectually mediated: the couple's relationship is tolerated on prescribed terms, and then exploited. The film condemns society's will to move automatically to 'acceptable' levels of life's rich colouring: the use of the mind to eat the soul.

6 *The Umbrellas of Cherbourg*
(Jacques Demy: France, 1964)

'Is it finished?' **(A customer of the Garage du Port-Aubin,**
and the first line of *The Umbrellas of Cherbourg*)

The previous chapters concentrate on the way arrangements
of colour express the thematic, intellectual, and emotional
designs of a particular narrative film. In the 'simple' stories
of *Written on the Wind* and *Fear Eats the Soul*, patterns of
demonstrative colour lead to probing accounts of the films'
and characters' complex personalities. In *Three Colours: White*
and *The Green Ray*, the palette infuses and is infused by the
sensibility of the central protagonist. In the latter film, the
designs are delicately indeterminate, restrained yet lightly
playful. A playful approach to colour and meaning in *Equinox
Flower* means that combinations of red objects may appear
as fun-but-empty graphic resemblances. However, they are
also open to an interpretation that links them to the film's
themes. This final chapter introduces a different fit to colour
and meaning's style–subject relationship. It addresses a
narrative film that involves more abstract and non-figurative
uses of colour. The intense colours in *The Umbrellas of Cherbourg* often meet the film's storylines (and we will investigate
what happens when they do). Equally, though, the colourful
arrays also spin and soar away, performing a dramatic dance
of their own.

Following Adrian Martin's article 'Delirious Enchantment', *The Umbrellas of Cherbourg* is a good example of 'a
cinema in which shapes [and] colours ... matter every bit as
much as faces, settings, dialogue, and dramatic plot happen-
ings.'[67] Martin continues, 'the complex of shapes and colours
... might be considered as the abstract-art side of cinema as a
pictorial medium. And when that complex is put into motion
through time, it's also a matter of the cinema's affinity with
music, music as a language of feeling and form.'[68] 'Shapes
and colours', 'music as a language of feeling and form': this
film brings these elements together in grand compositions.
The imposing arrangements tip the film towards abstraction.
Rather than becoming coldly intellectual (as is often seen to
be the case with abstract impulses in the cinema), the effect
leads towards, not away from, feeling. As Martin notes:

> Abstraction in film can also be full of drama, and that is
> because it involves tension ... Tension and timing in film are
> ways of relaying, re-routing, displacing and transforming
> emotion. That emotion can go through the line of a form, a
> split-second's flicker or perturbation, a shift in values of light
> or colour – as much as through a face, a word or an entirely
> identified, personalised human action.[69]

It is the dramatic tensions of colour, music, form, and feeling presented in *The Umbrellas of Cherbourg* that this chapter
seeks to bring out.

To be clear: the film has a solid narrative framework. It
presents us with an intricate story of romantic love in a
French town. Drawing on the forms of the classical Hollywood musical, the film intertwines plots of amorous esca-
pades and domestic or professional duty with song. Likewise,
it revels in applying the same explosive saturations of colouring used in such Golden Age Hollywood musical extrava-
ganzas as *Meet Me in St Louis* (Vincente Minnelli, 1944) and
Singin' in the Rain (Stanley Donen and Gene Kelly, 1952).[70]
At the same time, *The Umbrellas of Cherbourg* plays fast and
loose with the rules of film musicals, of classical Hollywood,
and of narrative cinema itself. As Peter Kemp observes:

> For starters, although its creator, punnily [sic] and poetically,
> defines his work's special nature as 'un film en chanté', as in
> a film that is done in song, *Les Parapluies de Cherbourg* isn't
> truly a filmusical [sic], let alone a celluloid opera, popera or even
> poperetta. The entirely-sung-through plotline ... is performed as
> essentially recitative, except for a few, longer, more melodically
> soaring stretches of composer Michel Legrand's major 'lovers'
> motif ... So, most of what we hear on the soundtrack is the equiv-
> alent not of arias or of highlighted, tuneful ditties but a jazzily
> scored mesh of the 'in-between' bits that lead up, and into, and
> on from, those 'bigger' routines in operas and musicals.[71]

The film combines aspects and conventions from film musicals, opera, and operettas, whilst adhering to none of the
above. It fuses jazz and orchestral designs of classical music
to mix the freewheeling, improvisatory forms of one, and the
precise arrangements of the other.

Rather than presenting a fantastical world of high living to
match the riches of its soaring melodies, the film keeps its
feet firmly on the ground. It tells tales of humdrum experience, as workaday (at base level) as those of the British New
Wave. As the title of Jonathan Rosenbaum's article on the
film declares, *The Umbrellas of Cherbourg* sings 'Songs in
the Key of Everyday Life'.[72] Geneviève (Catherine Deneuve)
works in the family umbrella shop. Her lover Guy (Nino
Castelnuovo) is a car mechanic who must leave for military
service. As Geneviève falls pregnant, and after pleas from her
hard-up mother, she agrees to marry a diamond salesman.
Guy and Geneviève meet only briefly once more, without
reconciliation. Rosenbaum suggests that the clash of a grand
symphonic score with the measures and means of everyday
life comprises, 'a poetic exaltation of the ordinary'.[73] More
precisely, he notes that the film's sung dialogue is grounded
in the standard repetitions of common conversation, in, 'the
everyday speech patterns of the French, who trot out formu-
las on all sorts of occasions ... It's the most normal talk in the
world.'[74] The effect of these 'en-chanté' designs is to enchant
everyday language from within, drawing out and celebrating

its inherent musical qualities. At the same time, though, in highlighting the words we may use in daily life, the musical phrasing sometimes hits a more downbeat note, emphasising empty repetitions and mechanistic verbal expressions (like 'Have a nice day').

The heightened colour schemes inspire similarly conflicting feelings. The lush designs burst with so much emotion, celebrating life's bright pleasures. At the same time, their presence in this film's world places the mundane lives of the characters in stark relief. As Rosenbaum describes, '[the] heightening of visual detail is the counterpart of the heightening of emotions and the sharpening of form achieved by setting the dialogue to music.'[75] In turn, colours and music 'create a powerful emotional intensification that perfects or contradicts the banality of the dialogue'.[76] Perfects or contradicts: the film's sumptuous aural and visual designs slide with and against the workings of the characters' lives.

It is in their relationship with music that the displays of colour often slip out of synchronicity with the story. Sylvie Lindeperg and Bill Marshall note how, in *The Umbrellas of Cherbourg*, 'we witness optical and sound situations realized by coloured set-descriptions which no longer extend into actions but into songs, producing in some sense an "unhooking", a "discrepancy" of the action.'[77] There is a further divergence. Although the film's colours create internal harmonies and motifs as elaborate as those of the music, the two do not necessarily always match. In some instances, the colour schemes 'unhook' in terms of tone, moving away from or against the mood of the action *and* the music. Nothing quite fits. (In its very first line, the film asks, asks itself, the question 'is it finished?') For Rosenbaum, everything 'fails to cohere into a strong melodic line'.[78] Kemp's phrasing also echoes here, as we are presented with 'a jazzily scored mesh' of different elements. On some occasions, certain colours coordinate with the characters' actions, a narrative detail, the music, or just each other. On others, particular shapes and colours take control, play a virtuoso solo, opening up a motif that is adopted by the film's world, wholly or in part, or drops out of the picture after making its mark like a trumpet's held note. There is also the film's relationship with painting to consider. For example, Kemp claims the 'surrounding environs and wall-papered interiors' of *The Umbrellas of Cherbourg* 'often resemble Matisse and Dufy canvases come magically and movingly to life, right down to a kind of vibrantly two-dimensional perspectivity.'[79] A comparison with aspects of Kandinsky's painting and writing appears equally valid. Kandinsky's thoughts on 'the language of form and colour' in pictorial art come close to Martin's belief in the abstractly dramatic possibilities of shape, colour, and music in film. Without having to submit to Kandinsky's collective thesis on 'the spiritual', the passage below can be seen to chime with this film's feelings and forms:

> The adaptability of forms, their organic but inward variations, their motion in the picture, their inclination to material or abstract, their mutual relations, either individually or as parts of a whole; further, the concord or discord of the various elements of a picture, the handling of groups, the combinations of veiled and openly expressed appeals, the use of rhythmical or unrhythmical, of geometrical or non-geometrical forms, their contiguity or separation – all these things are the material for counterpoint in painting. But so long as colour is excluded, such counterpoint is confined to black and white. Colour provides a whole wealth of possibilities of her own, and when combined with form, yet a further series of possibilities.[80]

Like Kandinsky's paintings, *The Umbrellas of Cherbourg* highlights the powerful aesthetic properties of colour.[81] Aspects of 'concord' and 'discord' are intrinsic to the film's designs. Unlike later Kandinsky pieces, it stays within the realm of representational forms and colours. Yet, the intensity, range, and placement of colours on display shift the meaning of any given scenario. The 'contiguity or separation' of the palette, music, settings, and dramatic thrust of each scene create a 'further series of possibilities', conveying different sensations.

Prelude

Umbrellas opens in a whirling overture. By design, the title
sequence encourages us to see the world in the abstract.
Long shots of Cherbourg harbour bookend the scene, glowing in the evening dusk. It is the film's first playful conceit.
The initial view, an establishing shot of an actual location,
raises expectations for a realistic (or, at the very least, conven-
tional) set of scenarios, only for such an outlook to be quickly
turned over. The Turner-pink skies over the water hint at a
more opaque approach to the world, at an interest in tricks
of the light. A boat-horn blurts an invitation for the musical score to begin. A flute plays the film's main theme. The
wistful melody drifts to join the hazy clouds. Rising up and
over, the camera slowly cranes from the harbour to the street
below. The motion tilts the vista, makes it askew. The ordinary things of the world appear at an angle. Completing its
pivot, the camera settles on a view high over the city. Seen
from above, the pavement becomes a blank canvas: a board of˙
dull brown and slate-grey tablets onto which brighter trickles
gradually collect.

The film begins to paint on prime colours in perky dots
and criss-cross lines. The bird's eye view picks out the cheeky
red tuft of a sailor-boy's hat as he holds his flame-haired

6.1 *The Umbrellas of Cherbourg* (Jacques Demy, 1964)

companion. A sunny-jacketed cyclist pushes his bicycle across the diagonal yellow line of a street marking. The wheels stick to the track as precisely as a paint-roller. Suddenly, the heavens open. Rain streams down in fine threads: more diagonal streaks. The pouring water brings greater swathes of colour. The action is reminiscent of Pollack's favoured approach to painting, dripping colour onto a blank canvas. As the rain tips down, passers-by open umbrellas [see plate 33]. From above, the umbrellas become staccato shots of brightness, unfurling like flowers. Circles and dashes of colour puddle together. A red umbrella unfastens to open a pattern of ruby shapes. A sailor's navy umbrella glides by the baby-blue lettering of the credits, while a red pram rolls on. A lilac mix of umbrellas floats down-screen in a horizontal row as the film's title appears in hot-pink. Throughout the parade, the musical theme tinkles in the rain. The sequence closes on a straight line of black umbrellas, ending on a darker note.

The movement through the sequence recalls some of Kandinsky's principles for counterpoint in painting: 'the adaptability of forms ... their motion in the picture ... their mutual relations, either individually or as parts of a whole ... the concord or discord of the various elements'. In its use of geometric planes, arcs and strokes, *Umbrellas'* credits bring to mind the painter's compositions, 'in which patches of colour and gestures of the brush are intended to carry the work's meaning directly to the spectator.'[82] Whether facing Kandinsky's *Transverse Line* (1923), or *Umbrellas'* first oblique colour-coda, 'the spectator has to feel his way into the composition.'[83] Both artist and film are concerned with the mutability of colour's adherence to the material and abstract. These first few moments present sharp lines and deep colours in rounded forms, and, at the same time, bits and pieces of ordinary life: bicycles and umbrellas. Another, more modern, artist's comments are also pertinent here. In interview, Jessica Stockholder exclaims, 'I like there to be places where the material is forgotten, but I also love to force a meeting of abstraction with material. Colour is very good at this, always ready to assert itself as independent from the material.'[84] While the rest of the film settles into a less immediately abstract setting than that of its opening tableau, it holds true to the first frames' interest in colour, in its ability to merge non-figurative and figurative aspects. As the opening swing from city vista to trippy canvas breaks free from the material, it encapsulates colour's mischievous place in the film, spreading and scurrying in a tilted world-view.

The title sequence also encourages a negotiation of the 'mutual relations' between parts and the whole. The opening sequence plays out as a self-contained sketch of the bigger picture: same but different, an extract of its colourful plans. An inquisitive gallery-goer may scan a Kandinsky, seizing upon particular lines and dots before stepping back to make sense of the piece in its entirety. Similarly, each slash, circle, or jab of the film credits' colours demands individual and collective attention. *Umbrellas* develops the game by breaking its story's temporal structure into three parts and multiple sub-sections of months and years. For example, there is the 'First Part: The Departure'; 'November 1957'; 'Second Part: The Absence'; 'February 1958'; 'March 1958'; and 'Third Part: The Return'. In the spirit of the film's splintered framework, the following reading focuses on separate patterns of shapes and colours that often coexist in the frame, looking at aspects of 'concord' and 'discord' in *Umbrellas*' fragmented designs.

Rhythm and blues

A blast of jazz lifts us into the world of the film. Riffs drift through the whole picture, but are particularly associated with Guy's place of work, the Garage du Port-Aubin. We will stop here twice. The film's soundtrack fills the busy workshop with jazz forms: variations, improvisations, constantly shifting patter. Yet it takes a while to find its groove. Initially, as the camera holds on the shop's exterior from across the street, there are bright flares of colour and music. A flurry of pastel umbrellas crosses hot splashes of light over wet tiles.

The garage fascia is bright red. There is a sense of things firing up, stepping into gear. The motor-shop's red neon-sign blinks into life in synch with the first trumpet's parp. Yet as we enter the shop, although the music continues to soar, colours become more muted, downbeat, black, and blue. The mellifluous energy of a jazz bop bashes into a more mechanical world. While the mix of jumping music, stifled colour, and stark words at first appears discordant, it suddenly settles into strokes. Gentle verbal and visual traffic flows into the to-and-fro of everyday life. A soft-shoe musical rhythm meets the pace of passing chatter: 'It's normal'; 'Thank you'; 'Thank you'. Figures pad across the garage floor: a customer in, a customer out. Guy strolls to the street entrance, taking an admiring glance at the pools and swirls of livelier colours. It is refreshing: a few splashes of rain hit his face. However, a duller task soon tugs him back, as the lumbering load of a pitch-black car rolls in for service. The eagle-eyed viewer spies the car's owner as Roland Cassard (Marc Michel), Geneviève's rival suitor. This car's entry adds a stroke of black humour and keeps Guy in automatic mode, driving him back inside.

The tone changes, gets jaunty again, when Guy joins his fellow-workers out back. Here in the locker-room the jazz skips and shuffles a little more freely, in step with the colleagues' banter away from the boss. They are still at work, so the mood is still blue, but clocking-off comes soon, bringing cheer. Throughout the room and in the workers' clothes blues predominate, clustering in different shades, single parts of a cohesive collective. The patchwork design of Guy's sweater – indigo, navy, sapphire jags and stripes – brings them all together. Colour, soundtrack, and chatter combine in variations on a theme. The men gather around the steely-blue bar of a wash-pipe. A melody of greetings slips into moments of virtuosity. Each worker notes his favourite artistic pursuit: theatre, movies, dancing. They take turns, performing a little celebration of their chosen pastime, offering a spin, line, or chord, before returning to the main bar.

A second and final trip to Guy's garage is notable as the
venue for his emotional breakdown. This time, the discordance between happy squawks of jazz and more mechanical notes does not give way. The workspace looks sickly (a
queasy yellow window peels in the corner) and words are
hurled like bricks: 'Foucher?'; 'Foucher!'; 'The boss wants
you'; 'Shit'. Guy's malaise is treated with contempt in the
clinical whites of the boss's office. (An unhappy customer
is asked, 'Complete check-up on the twenty-sixth, right sir?')
Badmouthing gets Guy fired. His temper threatens to tip the
moment over into violence. The boldest coloured object in
the room, a heavy green filing cabinet, looks set to topple. He
cannot contain himself; peeling off his blues, Guy tumbles
into the too-white street, anger giving way to emptiness.

Clashes

Umbrellas' colours sometimes rhyme with the characters'
personalities, but there are also clashes between them. The
film sets up two related patterns of discordance. It pits characters against each other in the colour of their clothing and
temperament. More oddly, it sets a scene's tone against that
of the décor. The former effect prickles the initial views of
Geneviève with her mother, Madame Emery (Anne Vernon).
This is our first time in the family's umbrella shop. A close
shot caresses Geneviève's blonde hair as she embraces Guy in
the street. Pretty Delft-style tiles form a backdrop to the kiss,
white tickled with blue. A cut rudely splices these smooth
light surfaces with the deep purples of the shop's interior.
Plum walls boast of the store's covetable wares: umbrellas
tilted on display. Browns, blues, and blacks jostle in clashing
strips. The umbrellas' harsh diagonal stems recall musical
notes scratched on a bar, or cracks in a glass. Now the camera
tracks to window panels broken up with dangling hooks. The
neat clutter smashes up the space of the shop. This is an
orderly place, and its orderliness produces a sense of underlying anxiety, especially for Geneviève.

The mother's appearance is of an elegant yet fussy presence. She glides across the room to a new customer while dabbing at her prim hair-do. Her shawl is a delicate blue, with a twitching fringe. The music rises in orchestral sunbursts, but the décor's designs are too busy to notice. Geneviève re-enters the shop. In the first meeting point of mother and daughter, the film explores aspects of closeness and friction. At this time, the colours of their clothes coalesce in yellow and blue pastels. Later, there are stronger clashes, of red, pink, and green in spats and spots, especially in the family apartment's hectic frescos. Yet initially, the film keeps them close. Mother clucks 'where were you?' moving over to fuss while Geneviève turns away, twirling a frond of hair. There is a faint air of aggravation to their turning bodies, in bumping elbows and pernickety fiddling. Physical proximity emphasises their mannerisms' similarities. Brushing close, the two women rub each other the wrong way. A stack of red boxes stands in between, boldly volunteering to separate them. Looking longingly out of the window at Guy cycling away, Geneviève traces her hand over the boxes. She finds some solace in the shop. At the same time, her duties hold her from a more exciting life, stock-still.

Later moments present emphatic blocks of colour, dense backgrounds that play against the pitch of the scene. As

6.2 *The Umbrellas of Cherbourg* (Jacques Demy, 1964)

Guy rides home, plans of an evening's dancing swerve into awkward displays. Bike and camera track past a mauve wall [see plate 34]. Reminiscent of a Miró print, the surface is an abstraction of purple and stinging bumblebee shades. Its crying design is better placed later as the lovers bid farewell. Here, given a weirdly fractious glance by the camera, it is a fright. Guy gently props his cycle in an enclave of toxic green: an obnoxious spatter of slime-green on crusting walls. Although he skips nimbly up the steps and the music keeps on bouncing, the setting is jaded. A mouldy olive colour carries inside the apartment, and mixes with bold reds and blues. Brash designs clash terribly against Guy's gentle greeting of Aunt Élise (Mireille Perrey). Conversation carries on in lightly polite chatter, but soon Élise weeps, perhaps out of happiness for Guy's love of Geneviève, perhaps not. The music swoons a little, but the walls' thick slabs of green and red are blankly one-note.

Umbrellas delights in such perversions of mood. Consider the young lovers' date. Everything starts so nicely. As Guy gets ready for the evening ahead, the colour of his work-shirt blends with his bedroom's blue walls. He picks out a pink shirt. A cut glides forward in time to the happy meeting. Geneviève's dashing coral jacket marries well with the shade of Guy's shirt. Soon, though, things come a little undone. In the opera box, Guy pricks his finger on the pink coat's pins. They laugh it off, just as *Carmen* reaches its sad crescendo. Off to the dance hall, and a flirty tango ushers them inside. Played on an accordion, the chirpy tune's flow sometimes hiccups and squelches. More unsettling still is the baroque depths of the room's redness [see plate 35]. A purportedly cheerful place filled with tipsy revellers, the nightspot drowns in bloody overstatement. (The venue's history reaches an appropriately seamy conclusion. On Guy's return from war, it flaunts its true colours as a full-blown bordello). While seemingly jolly and in love, the couple cannot relax in this space: they spin into a dance, then sit, pecking at each other in nipping kisses. While the lovers sip lemonade and say they are content, the fat gush of red décor squashes out any room for comfort.

A later moment is even stranger. Guy finally recognises his true love for Madeleine (Ellen Farner), Aunt Élise's long-suffering aide. Time passes, and Élise dies. In her will, she leaves some money to Guy. He joins Madeleine sitting in the sun outside a bar, to give news of his financial arrangements of Élise's estate. *Umbrellas* sets up a scene of settlement. The musical soundtrack points the way to harmony. The film seals the deal in verbal exclamation ('now everything is settled'), and in an accepted marriage proposal. However, background colours skew the 'happily ever after' design into a contrary expression of uncertainty. Late, Guy almost runs past his new love, and it is easy to see why. In an orange dress, Madeleine all but disappears into the burnt-amber backdrop of the bar's facade, as if sinking in clay. The predominant colouring, whilst imposing, is indeterminate: orangey, yellowish-brown. The tone of the meeting becomes uncertain, too, as discussions turn from the 'great news' to 'poor Élise' to Geneviève, the ghost of romance past. Emotional states become ambiguous: 'Are you happy?' 'I am not unhappy'. Like the bordello-red, the surrounding colour swamps the moment. Textures of nearby objects also complicate the tone. Guy nestles by some charming and thorny white roses. Madeleine sits next to blue frosted glass, delicate, brittle, and opaque. Although the soundtrack is dreamy, *Umbrellas* presents a smudged muddle of romantic compromise.

Shifts

Sometimes sudden cuts into diverse colour schemes cause quick dislocations. One supercharged example: pacing the apartment, Madame Emery squabbles with Geneviève about how to tackle their shock financial hardship. Coming round to the idea that she could sell off her jewellery ('After all, a jewel is just a jewel'), Madame whisks across the room towards her boudoir. As she moves, her bold red dress cuts against the vertical pink and green stripes of the living room's wallpaper. The music scores the movement: a drumstick plinks across xylophone keys. Pausing for a beat in the hallway and in front of the mirror she asks 'Should I change my hairstyle?' before stepping into the bedroom.

The clean pastel wallpaper stripes are instantly replaced with a deep red Victorian phantasmagoria. Gold curlicues and gilded cabbage-sized flowers flock across the walls. Whilst the mother's dress matches the wallpaper and equally heavy red drapes, Geneviève's entrance in the bedroom adds further fury to the design: a shock of pink in a red sea.

The shifts shape into an overbearing moment that both coheres with the narrative designs and threatens to disrupt the film's world order. The corresponding reds of Madame Emery and the bedroom express a sense of firm resolve (yes, we *will* sell the jewels). But then she cries, 'Come on! After all, it's not that pretty' and there is the suggestion of uncertainty: that no one will want such gaudy things, that the very fabrication of such an idea is inherently vulgar. The rapid change in colours creates a searing visual jolt. As we gradually become accustomed to the film's odd world, adjusting to the mix of naturalistic dialogue, everyday settings, and carnival colouring, *Umbrellas* pulls away the rug. The film is keen to shake us up from time to time, stopping us settling into the cinematic fabric, pointing to its fabrication. In this instance – the cut of a dress across wallpaper, a move into different rooms – quick changes strengthen an already intense experience. The film's insistent colour schemes compel us to question their presence. They too shout 'Come on! After all, it's not that pretty'.

Pop

The film is nearly over. We have reached the last fragment: December 1963. The final moments offer melancholy signals of closure and change. Madeleine gives a response to the film's first question – 'Is it finished?' – saying yes, 'I have finished'. There is an establishing shot of a new location, Guy's garage, looking pristine amidst white drifts. The opening sequence's oily rainfall, bringing to life dancing circles of colourful umbrellas, now freezes into snow. (We move back to the realm of *Three Colours: White*, to a place of blank settlement.) On the garage front and a prominently placed Esso sign, the previous lurid designs taper to three colours: blue, white, and red [see plate 36]. The three colours also echo those of the French flag. Across the rest of the film, intense and surprising tones often play discordantly against a scene's dramatic trajectory. Brightly painted everyday objects have moved *Umbrellas* towards the non-representational, stressing colour's ability to mutate appearance. Here, colour reclaims a fixed relationship with specific symbols: the Esso trademark, the national flag. In the end, perhaps with more than a touch of regret, the film's world and its inhabitants sink back into conformity.

In artistry and attitude, the final moments differ from everything that has gone before. The film balances two suggestions. First, allusions to Pop Art replace an earlier affinity with the work of painters such as Pollack, Kandinsky, and Miró. As with the Esso sign, the film ultimately draws nearer to the true resemblance of things of the world. At the same time, the act of placing any item in a film, however ordinary, can change our perspective of its aesthetic object. As with pop-art portraits of Coke bottles, bananas, or dollar bills, the Esso sign's appearance alters when shown in the frame, signifies in another way. Secondly, for Guy and Madeleine, life has changed dramatically as they now have a son, François (Hervé Legrand). The closing sequence's colouring has a child-like quality: crude, simplistic, and lively. Inside the garage, the camera tracks left to reveal a brightly decorated Christmas

6.3 *The Umbrellas of Cherbourg* (Jacques Demy, 1964)

tree. Little François taps a drumstick on an oil tin, sporting
a multicoloured Native American head-dress. Madeleine is
planning a trip to town as, 'The boy would like to see the
toys in the shop windows.' Everything is designed around
the child. The outer shell of the garage uncannily resembles
Guy's toy version, previously glimpsed on his bedroom floor.
Whereas there is a cheerful innocence to François' toys and
games, the notion of a crude childhood plaything replicated
as an adult reality is quietly unsettling. The building's form as
a cinematic creation, its plastics, enhances this feeling. A toy

6.4 *The Umbrellas of Cherbourg* (Jacques Demy, 1964)

garage becomes a life-sized model in uncomplicated colours, the inflated scale making it strange. Equally, in the garage shop, uniform red rows of Esso oil cans are as mundane and arresting as a painted likeness of Campbell's soup. The last few moments of *The Umbrellas of Cherbourg* contain a sense of completion, but also a shock of the new. In two related approaches – a pop-art style and an emphasis on child's play – the film looks at the world with fresh eyes.

In turn, Geneviève's unexpected appearance brings to mind aspects of Warhol's Monroe. From her chauffeur-driven car, she glides into the garage, blonde hair fixed high, with all the trappings of commodity culture. She has changed and yet, somehow, she remains the same. For Guy, she retains a magical trace of her former self. The way these two characters finally present themselves again to each other – hello, goodbye – is both mechanically contrived and heartfelt. It is a reproduction of an earlier golden age, brightly tinted but tinged with sadness.

Afterword

Paying attention to particularities, relationships, and patterns of style allows the viewer to unlock and appreciate the concerns of a film. Looking at how a small group of films handles colours, setting out descriptions of different palettes and designs, this book has engaged in a process of interpretation. Each chapter has worked to find words that match the experience of viewing a dab, flourish, shade, flash, or wash of colour in cinematic moments. Getting into the details of the films' colourful arrangements, the book has offered a series of close readings. Deborah Thomas provides a useful definition of how the readings, while close, are not closed:

> The readings can most usefully be understood as sustained meditations grounded in the detailed specifics of their texts. At their best, such accounts invite those to whom they are offered to revisit the films and see for themselves, enriching their own experiences with new depth and bringing significant details to their attention in fresh and productive ways, while ultimately encouraging such viewers to make up their own minds as to how true to their own experiences of the film the readings may be, and how illuminating and important the issues that they raise.[85]

Following Thomas, raising some details of the films and of colour in film, the interpretations offer invitations rather than solutions. As Perkins notes:

No intra-textual interpretation ever is or ever could be a proof. Most often it is a description of aspects of the film with suggested understandings of some of the ways they are patterned. Rhetoric is involved in developing the description so that it evokes a sense of how, seen in this way, the film may affect us, or so that it invites participation in the pleasure of discovering the way in which various of the film's features hang together.[86]

As 'sustained meditations', the readings in this book have concentrated their attention not only on the 'detailed specifics of their texts', but also on one element within the specifics, on the way arrangements of colours 'hang together'. They have drawn on the tools of mise-en-scène criticism to attend to a stylistic feature that often bypasses textual analysis.

As one of the features of a film's composition, colour does not work alone. The meaning of an application of colour in a given moment relates to other points of style such as camerawork, editing, décor, performance, costume, music, sound, and lighting. As Perkins also reminds us, 'The specifically filmic qualities derive from the *complex*, not from any one of its components. What distinguishes film from any other media, and the fiction movie from other forms, is none of the elements but their combination, interaction, fusion.'[87] From the very first example of the twirled yellow feather in *The Green Ray* – an instance of gesture, colour, and texture working together – the readings have explored the coupling and contrast of stylistic elements, noting the interplay of one to the next.

Colour is a regular feature in the majority of modern narrative films. As such, it is easy to overlook its appearance, to take it for granted, or to wait for the moment when it announces its significance. Some films colour their worlds without involved, provocative, or profound arrangements, painting-by-numbers as it were. Others strongly assert the importance of certain colours at particular points of the story or for specific purposes. In its ability to emphasise moods and meanings, in its symbolic and dramatic impact, colour in film often makes direct statements or glosses key points.

This book has considered six films that understand and move beyond colour's blatancy. In *Written on the Wind*, the presence of colour is emphatic and enigmatic. The colourful displays of *Fear Eats the Soul* and *The Umbrellas of Cherbourg* are loud, but rather than blaring out crude messages, the assertive schemes complicate matters in precise measures. In *The Green Ray*, pale shades are eloquently diffuse. In *Equinox Flower*, limited ranges of red, black, and white designs become complex in their reappearance. *Three Colours: White* explores the intricacies of one colour's properties and associations. There are many more examples across cinema's vast spectrum.

Appendix A: DVD information

Krzysztof Kieślowski (director), *The Three Colours Trilogy*, Artificial Eye, ART 275 DVD (Region 2 PAL), distributed by WCL: World Cinema Limited, 2005.

Yasujiro Ozu (director), *The Ozu Collection: Volume Three* (*Tokyo Twilight; Equinox Flower; Good Morning*), Tartan DVD, 3 x DVD9 (Region 2 PAL), distributed by WCL: World Cinema Limited, 2006.

Eric Rohmer (director), *The Green Ray*, 'The Eric Rohmer Collection', Arrow Films (Region 2 PAL), Freemantle Home Entertainment, 2003.

Douglas Sirk (director), *Written on the Wind*, Universal Pictures DVD, DVD 821-993-6 11 (Region 2 PAL), Universal Pictures (UK) Ltd, 2005.

Rainer Werner Fassbinder (director), The Rainer Werner Fassbinder Foundation Presents *Fear Eats the Soul*, Arrow Films (Region 2 PAL), Südwestrundfunk, 2006.

Jacques Demy (director), *The Umbrellas of Cherbourg*, Optimum World DVD (Region 2 PAL), Optimum Releasing, 2005.

Appendix B: Colour in film
– a timeline

1664–66 Isaac Newton discovers that white light is composed of different colours

1794 First Panorama opens: the forerunner of the
movie house invented by Robert Barker

1841 William Henry Talbot patents the Calotype
process: the first negative-positive photographic
process making possible the first multiple copies

1864 George Eastman invents flexible, paper-based
photographic film

1895 Thomas Edison makes the hand-painted work
Anabelle's Dance for Kinetoscope viewers

1902 *A Trip to the Moon* (director, George Méliès) –
pioneering experimentation in colour tinting

1903 *The Great Train Robbery* (director, Siegmund
Lubin) – each sequence dyed one colour to match
a shot's mood or activity

1906 British pioneers Edward R. Turner and George
Albert Smith introduce Kinemacolor

1915–21 Development of Technicolor by Herbert Kalmus
and Daniel Comstock

1916 *Intolerance* (director, D. W. Griffith) – uses the
colour stencilling of Pathécolor

1917 *Joan the Woman* (director, Cecil B. DeMille) – uses
Handschiegl Color

Our Navy (director, George A. Dorsey) – uses
William Van Doren Kelley's Prizma Color
1918   *Cupid Angling* (director, Leon F. Douglass) – uses
Naturalcolor
1925   *Greed* (director, Erich von Stroheim)
1926   *The Black Pirate* (director, Albert Parker) – uses
Technicolor
1929   Eastman Kodak introduce pre-tinted black-and-
white film stock Sonochrome
1931   Louis Dufay introduces Dufay Color
1932   *Flowers and Trees* (director, Burt Gillett for Walt
Disney) – first animated feature to use Technicolor
Creation of the CineColor Corporation (creating
the Multicolor system)
1935   Eastman Kodak markets Kodachrome film
Becky Sharp (director, Rouben Mamoulian) –
Technicolor
1938   *The Adventures of Robin Hood* (director, Michael
Curtiz) – Technicolor
1939   *Gone with the Wind* (director, Victor Fleming) –
Technicolor
The Wizard of Oz (director, Victor Fleming) –
Technicolor
1943   *Münchhausen* (director, Josef von Báky) –
Agfacolor
1946   *A Matter of Life and Death* (director, Michael
Powell and Emeric Pressburger) – Technicolor
sections
1949   *Jour de fête* (director, Jacques Tati) – filmed in
Thomsoncolor, originally released in black-and-
white, colour copy restored in 1995
1950   Kodak introduces Eastmancolor
1951   *An American in Paris* (director, Vincente Minnelli)
– Technicolor
1954   *Brigadoon* (director, Vincente Minnelli) – Ansco
Color

1958	*Vertigo* (director, Alfred Hitchcock) – Technicolor
1959	*Ben-Hur* (director, William Wyler) – Technicolor
1963	Polaroid introduces instant colour film
1964	*Red Desert* (director, Michelangelo Antonioni)
1968	*The Colour of Pomegranates* (director, Sergei Parajanov)
1971	*McCabe and Mrs Miller* (director, Robert Altman)
1973	*Don't Look Now* (director, Nicolas Roeg)
1974	*The Godfather* (director, Francis Ford Coppola) – resurrects the use of Technicolor
1977	*Suspiria* (director, Dario Argento) – Technicolor
1980	*Heaven's Gate* (director, Michael Cimino)
1982	*Sophie's Choice* (director, Alan Pakula)
1983	*Rumble Fish* (director, Francis Ford Coppola)
1985	Pixar introduces the digital image processor
	The Purple Rose of Cairo (director, Woody Allen)
1988	*Wings of Desire* (director, Wim Wenders)
1989	*The Icicle Thief* (director, Maurizio Nichetti)
1991	*Kafka* (director, Steven Soderbergh)
1993	*Schindler's List* (director, Steven Spielberg)
	Blue (director, Derek Jarman)
1998	*Pleasantville* (director, Gary Ross)
1999	*Kikujiro* (director, Takeshi Kitano)
2002	*Hero* (director, Yimou Zhang)
	Punch-Drunk Love (director, Paul Thomas Anderson)
2005	*Sin City* (director, Frank Miller and Robert Rodriguez)
2008	*WALL-E* (director, Andrew Stanton)
2009	*Avatar* (director, James Cameron) – uses advanced 3-D technology

Notes

1 S. Neale, *Cinema and Technology: Image, Sound, Colour* (London: BFI, 1985).

2 A. Dalle Vacche and B. Price (eds), *Color: the Film Reader* (London: Routledge, 2006).

3 W. Everett (ed.), *Questions of Colour in Cinema: From Paintbrush to Pixel* (*New Studies in European Cinema*, 6, Peter Lang Publications, 2007).

4 S. Higgins, *Harnessing the Technicolor Rainbow: Color Design in the 1930s* (University of Texas Press, 2008).

5 R. Dyer, *Only Entertainment* (London: Routledge, 1992), p. 22.

6 *Ibid.*, p. 18.

7 D. Bordwell and K. Thompson, *Film Art: An Introduction* (Longman, 1979), p. 75.

8 David Batchelor explores some of the preconceptions and intolerances that surround colour and colour-studies in *Chromophobia* (London: Reaktion Books, 2000).

9 S. Melville, 'Colour has not yet been named: objectivity in deconstruction', in Peter Brunette and David Wills (eds), *Deconstruction and the Visual Arts: Art, Media, Architecture* (Cambridge: Cambridge University Press, 1993), p. 45.

10 For example, Derek Schilling notes how 'judgements of Rohmer's work have not been uniformly kind. It has been qualified as elitist, coldly intellectual, repetitive in its situations and themes, and downright exasperating in its garrulousness and often precious tone ... This is a cinema of visual understatement and, admittedly, verbal excess, where actors must scrupulously adhere to a text that

determines their character's very being.' He cautions, however, that 'there is always more to a Rohmer film than meets the ear.' D. Schilling, *Eric Rohmer* (Manchester: Manchester University Press, 2007), pp. 1–3.

11 J. Leigh, 'Reading Rohmer', in John Gibbs and Douglas Pye (eds), *Close-Up 02* (London: Wallflower Press, 2008), p. 85.

12 *Ibid.* Leigh offers a rare and valuable stylistic reading of three of Rohmer's films, paying particular attention to, 'his interest in daydreaming ... his depiction of movement and stasis ... [and] his use of colours'.

13 A comment by Derek Schilling bridges the two chapters. Drawing a contrast between Rohmer's understatement and melodrama, Schilling's overview is symptomatic of related critical postulations about Sirk: 'In the narrative cinema, style is often assumed to lie on the side of visible excess. It is the domain of the provocateur, the virtuoso, the formalist, the mannerist.' Schilling, *Eric Rohmer*, p. 90.

14 In '*Mise en scène* is dead, or The Expressive, The Excessive, The Technical and The Stylish', Adrian Martin examines the different 'economies' in film (and film criticism) 'between the elements of style and subject'. These economies comprise the way 'the themes, ideas, events, situations, meanings, understandings, attitudes of the fiction are served and expressed by the stylistic strategies.' *Continuum* 5, 2, (1990), 87–140.

15 J. Gage, *Colour and Meaning: Art, Science and Symbolism*, (London: Thames and Hudson, 1999), pp. 11–12.

16 For an example of normative claims to colour's relationship with culture, see M. Sahlins, 'Colours and Their Cultures', *Semiotics* 15, 1, (1975), 1–22.

17 W. Kandinsky, *Concerning the Spiritual in Art*, trans. M. T. H. Sadler (London: Tate Publishing, 2006), p. 77.

18 *Ibid.*

19 Hereafter the film title is abridged to *White*.

20 Kandinsky, *Concerning the Spiritual in Art*, p. 77.

21 H. Oiticica, extract from 'Cor, tempo e estrutura', *Jornal do Brasil* (26 November 1960); reprinted in H. Oiticica, *Hélio Oiticica* (Paris: Galerie nationale du Jeu de Paume/Rio de Janeiro – Projeto Hélio Oiticica/Rotterdam: Witte de With, 1992), pp. 34–5.

22 Kandinsky, *Concerning the Spiritual in Art*, p. 41.

23 Oiticica, 'Cor, tempo e estrutura', p. 35.

24 See, for example, R. Dyer, *White* (London and New York:

Routledge, 1997); G. A. Foster, *Performing Whiteness: Postmodern Re/ Constructions in the Cinema* (Albany, New York: State University of New York Press, 2003); M. A. Berger, *Sight Unseen: Whiteness and American Visual Culture* (University of California Press, 2005); D. Bernadi, *The Persistence of Whiteness: Race and Contemporary Hollywood Cinema* (Taylor and Francis, 2007); and H. Loyo, 'Blinding Blondes: Whiteness, Femininity and Stardom' in Everett (ed.), *Questions of Colour in Cinema*, pp. 179–96.

25 G. Andrew, *The Three Colours Trilogy* (London: BFI, 1998), p. 11.

26 T. Szczepanski, 'Kieślowski wobec Begmana', in M. Haltof, *The Cinema of Krzysztof Kieślowski: Variations on Destiny and Chance* (London: Wallflower, 2004), p. 124.

27 G. Andrew, *The Three Colours Trilogy*, p. 25.

28 *Ibid.*, p. 27

29 D. Turner, 'The Interiority of the Unknown Woman in Film', unpublished doctoral manuscript, University of Kent, 2006, p. 16. Thank you to David Turner for permission to include quotations from the thesis. Turner's thesis is an exploration and new figuration of Stanley Cavell's concept of the 'unknown woman' detailed in *Contesting Tears: The Hollywood Melodrama of the Unknown Woman* (Chicago and London: University of Chicago Press, 1996). Turner declares a pivotal distinction between his understanding of the concept and Cavell's: that whereas Cavell places emphasis on the woman's theatrical responses to unknownness (via, for example, choice of solitude and refusal of marriage), Turner's argument focuses on the woman's 'interiority' as unknown, and the film's expression of unknown interiority, rather than the woman's responses to it. Kieślowski's *White* draws aspects of both understandings together. Karol's wife Dominique presents theatrical responses to unknownness (separating physically and legally from her husband; in the final orchestration of hand gestures); the film, in whiteness and other constituents of its *mise-en-scène*, expresses the unknown interiority of both Dominique and (through his wife's lack of responsiveness) Karol. In tone and design, *White* can be understood as a contemporary, European reshaping of the 'comedy of remarriage' genre that informs Cavell's concept of the 'unknown woman'.

30 Andrew, *The Three Colours Trilogy*, p. 38.

31 *Ibid.*

32 Y. Ozu, in Shiguehiko Hasumi, *Kantoku Ozu Yasujiro* (Tokyo: Chikuma shobo, 1983) p. 222. Cited in D. Bordwell, *Ozu and the*

Poetics of Cinema (London: BFI, 1988), p. 83.

33 This also reflects Ozu's own stance to sound, first opposing
and then carefully integrating it as a stylistic element, with his first
'talking picture' being *The Only Son* (1936).

34 L. Brost, 'On Seeing Red: The Figurative Movement of Film
Colour', in Everett (ed.), *Questions of Colour in Cinema*, p. 127.

35 *Ibid.*, p. 132. Brost refers to correspondent 'hyperbolic'
appearances of red in *Black Narcissus* (Michael Powell and Emeric
Pressburger, 1947) and *Bigger than Life* (Nicholas Ray, 1956). Two
recent examples of films that feature this colour for the purpose of
emphatic figuration are *Schindler's List* (Steven Spielberg, 1993) and
The Sixth Sense (M. Night Shyamalan, 1999), the latter in its covert
(yet forceful) dramatic coding of red objects.

36 *Ibid.*, p. 131.

37 Bordwell, *Ozu and the Poetics of Cinema*, p. 123.

38 *Ibid.*, p. 111.

39 *Ibid.*, p. 350.

40 *Ibid.*, p. 123.

41 *Ibid.*, p. 350.

42 A. Klevan, *Disclosure of the Everyday: Undramatic Achievement
in Narrative Film* (Trowbridge: Flicks Books, 2000), p. 160.

43 *Ibid.*, p. 145.

44 Schilling, *Eric Rohmer*, p. 73.

45 Turner, 'The Interiority of the Unknown Woman in Film'.
Turner's thesis provides a detailed exploration of *The Green Ray*,
looking particularly at Delphine's 'trapped interiority'.

46 Addressing Delphine's cliff-top strolls in Biarritz, Leigh notes
that '*Le Rayon vert*'s use of Delphine's red coat alludes ... to 'Little
Red Riding Hood'. Rohmer's film hints that a part of Delphine imagines – that maybe a part of all of us imagines – that men are either
wolves or huntsmen and that there is a part of us that indulges such
daydreams.' Leigh, 'Reading Rohmer', p. 125.

47 For notes on the 'technology and development of three-colour
Technicolor', see Higgins, *Harnessing the Technicolor Rainbow*, pp.
23–32.

48 *Ibid.*, p. 1.

49 J. Gibbs, *Mise-en-Scène: Film Style and Interpretation* (London:
Wallflower, 2003), pp. 70–71. Internal citation, Thomas Elsaesser,
'Tales of Sound and Fury: Observations on the Family Melodrama',
Monogram 4, (1972), 7.

50 Dalle Vacche and Price (eds), *Color: the Film Reader*, pp. 11–12.

51 N. M. Kalmus, 'Color Consciousness', reprinted in Dalle Vacche and Price (eds), *Color: the Film Reader*, p. 46.

52 *Ibid.*, p. 26.

53 See for example M. Deutelbaum, 'Costuming and the Color System of *Leave Her to Heaven*', in Dalle Vacche and Price (eds), *Color: the Film Reader*, p. 161–9.

54 V. F. Perkins, 'Must we say what they mean? Film criticism and interpretation', *Movie* 34/35, (1990), 4.

55 For a detailed appraisal of all stylistic elements in the '21' sequence, see S. Peacock, 'A Magnified Meeting in *Written on the Wind* (Douglas Sirk, 1956)', in T. Brown and J. Walters (eds), *Approaching Moments in Film: History, Theory, Aesthetics* (London: BFI/Palgrave, forthcoming 2010).

56 R. Fassbinder, in 'Life Stories: R. W. Fassbinder in conversation with Peter W. Jansen', on the 2006 Arrow Films DVD of *Fear Eats the Soul*, copyright 1978 Südwestrundfunk.

57 D. Thomson, *The New Biographical Dictionary of Film* (4th edn, London: Little, Brown, 2002), p. 278.

58 *Ibid.*, p. 279.

59 See, for instance, Fassbinder's own testimony in his article 'Six Films by Douglas Sirk', trans. T. Elsaesser, in L. Mulvey and J. Halliday (eds), *Douglas Sirk* (Edinburgh: Edinburgh Film Festival, 1972), pp. 104–07. Two good recent examples are the Todd Haynes interview on the 2006 Arrow Films DVD of *Fear Eats the Soul*, and Jonathan Rosenbaum's blog entries on Fassbinder at www.jonathan-rosenbaum.com (accessed 8 September 2009).

60 See, for example, L. Cottingham, *Fear Eats the Soul* (London: BFI Film Classics, 2005), p. 50.

61 Thomson, *The New Biographical Dictionary of Film*, p. 278.

62 *Ibid.*

63 J. Savage, 'The Conscious Collusion of the Stare: The Viewer Implicated in Fassbinder's *Fear Eats the Soul*', reprinted as 'Production Notes by Julian Savage' in the 2006 Arrow Films DVD of *Fear Eats the Soul*, 'by permission of "Senses of Cinema."'

64 V. F. Perkins, *Film as Film: Understanding and Judging Movies* (London and New York: Da Capo Press, 1993 reprinted edition), pp. 84–85. Robin Wood offers a critique of Perkins' readings of colour in *Personal Views: Explorations in Film* (Detroit: Wayne State University Press, revised edition, 2006), pp. 32-35.

65 Perkins, *Film as Film*, p. 8 (emphasis in original).

66 'Life Stories: R. W. Fassbinder in conversation with Peter W. Jansen', on the Arrow Films DVD of *Fear Eats the Soul*. The italics are mine.

67 A. Martin, 'Delirious Enchantment', *Senses of Cinema* 01/5, www.sensesofcinema.com (accessed 10 May 2006).

68 *Ibid.*

69 *Ibid.*, p. 10.

70 *The Umbrellas of Cherbourg* employs the Eastmancolor range. It has also since been technically restored. As Sylvie Lindeperg and Bill Marshall note, '[In 1992] a specially restored version was released, based on three monochrome positive prints requested from the Éclair laboratories as a security measure by Demy in 1964, the trichrome selection process enabling a renewed combination of red, green and blue colour; the soundtrack was also of course painstakingly restored.' S. Lindeperg and B. Marshall, 'European Musical Forms: Time, History and Memory in *Les Parapluies de Cherbourg*', in B. Marshall and R. Stillwell (eds), *Musicals: Hollywood and Beyond* (London: Intellect Books, 2000), pp. 98–106. This chapter's reading comes from viewings of the DVD version of the restored print (see Appendix A).

71 P. Kemp, 'Stingin' in the Rain: *The Umbrellas of Cherbourg*', *Senses of Cinema* 01/16, www.sensesofcinema.com (accessed 16 May 2006). Internal citation, J. Boineau, *Les 100 Chefs-D'oeuvre Du Film Musical* (Marabout: Ailleur, 1998), p. 162.

72 J. Rosenbaum, 'Songs in the Key of Everyday Life: *The Umbrellas of Cherbourg*', in J. Rosenbaum, *Essential Cinema: On the Necessity of Film Canons* (Baltimore and London: The Johns Hopkins University Press, 2004), pp. 32–37.

73 *Ibid.*, p. 33.

74 *Ibid.*, pp. 33–34.

75 *Ibid.*, p. 36.

76 *Ibid.*

77 Lindeperg and Marshall, 'European Musical Forms: Time, History and Memory in *Les Parapluies de Cherbourg*', pp. 98–106.

78 Rosenbaum, 'Songs in the Key of Everyday Life', p. 36.

79 Kemp, 'Stingin' in the Rain'.

80 Kandinsky, *Concerning the Spiritual in Art*, pp. 65–66.

81 The film's title is hereafter abridged to *Umbrellas*.

82 N. Stangos (ed.), *Concepts of Modern Art: from Fauvism to Post-*

modernism (London: Thames and Hudson, 3rd edn 1995), p. 40.

83 *Ibid.*, p. 41.

84 J. Stockholder and L. Tillman, 'Lynne Tillman in Conversation with Jessica Stockholder', in B. Schwabsky, L. Tillman and L. Cooke, *Jessica Stockholder* (London: Phaidon Press, 1995), p. 10.

85 D. Thomas, *Reading Hollywood: Spaces and Meaning in American Film*, (London and New York: Wallflower Press, 2001), pp. 1–2.

86 Perkins, 'Must We Say What They Mean? Film Criticism and Interpretation', p. 4.

87 Perkins, *Film as Film*, p. 117 (emphasis in original).

Bibliography

Andrew, Geoff *The Three Colours Trilogy* (London: BFI 1998)

Batchelor, David *Chromophobia* (London: Reaktion Books 2000)

—— (ed.) *Colour: Documents of Contemporary Art* Cambridge MA: Whitechapel 2008)

Berger, Martin A. *Sight Unseen: Whiteness and American Visual Culture* (California: University of California Press 2005)

Bernadi, Daniel *The Persistence of Whiteness: Race and Contemporary Hollywood Cinema* (London: Routledge 2007)

Boineau, Jean-Marc *Les 100 Chefs-D'oeuvre Du Film Musical* (Marabout: Ailleur 1998)

Bordwell, David and Kristin Thompson *Film Art: An Introduction* (California: McGraw-Hill 1979)

——, *Ozu and the Poetics of Cinema* (London: BFI 1988)

Branigan, Edward 'The Articulation of Color in a Filmic System', *Wide Angle* 1/3, 1976, pp. 20–36

Brunette, Peter and David Wills (eds) *Deconstruction and the Visual Arts: Art, Media, Architecture* (Cambridge: (Cambridge University Press 1993)

Cavell, Stanley *The World Viewed: Reflections on the Ontology of Film* (Cambridge MA: Harvard University Press 1975 enlarged edition)

Cavell, Stanley *Contesting Tears: The Hollywood Melodrama of*

the Unknown Woman Chicago and (London: University of
Chicago Press 1996)

Cook, David A. *A History of Narrative Film* (New York, London:
W. W. Norton and Company 1990, 2nd edn)

Cooke, Lynne, Barry Schwabsky and Lynne Tilman *Jessica
Stockholder* (London: Phaidon Press 1995)

Cottingham, Laura *Fear Eats the Soul* (London: BFI Film
Classics 2005)

Dalle Vacche, Angela and Brian Price (eds) *Color: the Film
Reader* (London: Routledge 2006)

Durgnat, Raymond 'Colours and Contrasts', *Films and Film-
ing* 15/2, November 1968, pp. 58–62

Dyer, Richard *Only Entertainment* (London: Routledge 1992)

——, *White* (London and New York: Routledge 1997)

Everett, Wendy (ed.) *Questions of Colour in Cinema: From
Paintbrush to Pixel*, New Studies in European Cinema
NECS 6 (Oxford, Bern, Berlin, Frankfurt am Main, New
York, Wein: Peter Lang Publications 2007)

Foster, G. A *Performing Whiteness: Postmodern Re/Construc-
tions in the Cinema* (Albany, New York: State University of
New York Press 2003)

Gage, John *Colour and Meaning: Art, Science and Symbolism*
(London: Thames and Hudson 1999)

Gibbs, John *Mise-en-Scène: Film Style and Interpretation*
(London: Wallflower 2003)

Haltof, Marek *The Cinema of Krzysztof Kieślowski: Variations
on Destiny and Chance* (London: Wallflower 2004)

Higgins, Scott *Harnessing the Technicolor Rainbow: Color
Design in the 1930s* (Texas: University of Texas Press 2008)

Kandinsky, Wassily *Concerning the Spiritual in Art*, trans. M.
T. H. Sadler (London: Tate Publishing 2006)

Kemp, Peter 'Stingin' in the Rain: *The Umbrellas of Cherbourg*',
Senses of Cinema 01/16, 2001, http://archive.sensesof-
cinema.com/contents/cteq/01/16/umbrellas.html

Klevan, Andrew *Disclosure of the Everyday: Undramatic Achievement in Narrative Film* (Trowbridge: Flicks Books 2000)

Leigh, Jacob 'Reading Rohmer' *Close-Up 02* John Gibbs and

Douglas Pye (eds) (London: Wallflower Press 2008)

Lindeperg, Sylvie and Bill Marshall, 'European Musical Forms: Time, History and Memory in *Les Parapluies de Cherbourg' Musicals: Hollywood and Beyond* Bill Marshall and Robyn Stillwell (eds) (Exeter: Intellect Books 2000), pp. 98–106

Martin, Adrian *'Mise en scène* is dead, or The Expressive, The Excessive, The Technical and The Stylish' *Continuum* 5/2, 1992, pp. 87–140

——, 'Delirious Enchantment' *Senses of Cinema* 1/5, www.sensesofcinema.com/contents/00/5/index.html

Mulvey, Laura and Jon Halliday (eds) *Douglas Sirk* (Edinburgh: Edinburgh Film Festival 1972)

Neale, Steve *Cinema and Technology: Image, Sound, Colour* (London: BFI 1985)

Peacock, Steven 'A Magnified Meeting in *Written on the Wind' Approaching Moments in Film: History, Theory, Aesthetics* Tom Brown and James Walters (eds) (London: BFI/ Palgrave 2010)

Perkins, V. F. 'Must We Say What They Mean? Film Criticism and Interpretation' *Movie* 34/35, Winter 1990, pp. 1–6

——, *Film as Film: Understanding and Judging Movies* (London and New York: Da Capo Press 1993 reprinted edition)

Rosenbaum, Jonathan *Essential Cinema: On the Necessity of Film Canons* (Baltimore and London: The Johns Hopkins University Press 2004)

——, www.jonathanrosenbaum.com (accessed September 2009)

Ruskin, John *Selected Writings* (Oxford: Oxford University Press 2009)

Sahlins, Marshal 'Colours and Their Cultures' *Semiotics* 15/1, 1975, pp. 1–22

Schilling, Derek *Eric Rohmer* (Manchester: Manchester University Press 2007)

Slide, Anthony *The New American Film Industry: A Historical Dictionary* (London: Routledge, 1998)

Stangos, Nikos (ed.) *Concepts of Modern Art: from Fauvism to*

Postmodernism (London: Thames and Hudson, 3rd edn, 1995)

Tarantino, Quentin *Reservoir Dogs: The Complete Script* (London: Faber and Faber 1994)

Thomas, Deborah *Reading Hollywood: Spaces and Meaning in American Film* (London and New York: Wallflower Press 2001)

Thomson, David *The New Biographical Dictionary of Film* (London: Little, Brown 2002, 4th edn)

Turner, David 'The Interiority of the Unknown Woman in Film' (unpublished doctoral manuscript University of Kent 2006)

Wood, Robin *Personal Views: Explorations in Film* (Detroit: Wayne State University Press 2006, revised edn)

Zusak, Markus *The Book Thief* (London: Black Swan 2007)

Index